THE WISDOM OF
TUSCANY

THE WISDOM OF
TUSCANY

SIMPLICITY, SECURITY
& THE GOOD LIFE ~
MAKING THE TUSCAN LIFESTYLE YOUR OWN

FERENC MÁTÉ

W.W. NORTON   NEW YORK   LONDON

For our children

IBSN 978-0920256-68-8

The text in this book is composed in Adobe Garamond

Book design and composition by Candace Máté
Manufactured by R. R. Donnelley, U. S. A.

Albatross Books at
W. W. Norton & Company Inc., 500 Fifth Avenue, New York, NY 10110
http://www.wwnorton.com

W. W. Norton & Company Ltd., 10 Coptic Street, London WCA 1PU
  2 3 4 5 6 7 8 9 10

CONTENTS

APPENDIX

A LETTER TO THE READER

Dear Reader,

Tuscan wisdom I found nowhere written. With the exception of some proverbs, no slogans proclaim it, no songs laud its virtues; it seems instead to quietly surround you, to engulf you unnoticed like the warmth of a summer night. It is there in the tranquil landscape, the proud hill-towns, the vitality of Florentine art, the serenity of the paintings and buildings of Siena.

    But mostly it is expressed in la vita quotidiana, *daily life, in the encounters of Tuscans in the streets, cafes, shops, and open markets; in the bonds that hold people together—families, neighbors, communities and friends. And it is there in the quality of the craftsman's labors, the lovingly tended vineyards and olive groves, the lush vegetable gardens, the long daily meals, the crusty loaves of bread, the complex pasta sauces, the robustness of its wine.*

    I have no intention or pretensions to be a reverse De Tocqueville, but having spent one half of my life in Europe and the other in North America—my childhood in Hungary, my youth in Canada, years in California and New York, and the last twenty in Tuscany—I simply try to understand the startling differences between the two worlds. And while each has much to learn from the other, it appears more and more that the balance is swinging back toward old Europe, to Italy, and above all to Tuscany, where the epitome of "the good life" seems to reside. And more and more, the splendor of material wealth begins to pale when compared to the simple richness of daily Tuscan life.

So this book—sometimes rambling, always probing, now and then chaotic, but most often admiring—is, if anything, an attempt to remind us—remind me—of the boundless joy in living, the thrill of simple things, the daily celebrations, the pleasure that people bring, and the pleasure that we are capable of giving.

It is meant to awaken the Tuscan in us all.

Ferenc Máté
Montalcino, Italy
Summer, 2009

1 ~ A TUSCAN CHILDHOOD

*G*razietta is petite. She's just over five feet tall, but has such piercing eyes that they could hypnotize you, and a voice so clear and forceful it can pin you to a wall. Marching up and down the steep stone streets of our town, Montalcino, where she was born almost sixty years ago, she has the gait and spring of a girl still in her teens. She's very pretty. She ran her own hair salon all her life, which means she heard, mostly sooner than later, everything there was in town that was worth repeating. She is also one of our best-read and most articulate citizens, and she speaks with enormous passion about this place.

A fervent Tuscan, proud of her Etruscan blood, she says with dignity, "We're not like the Romans. They chipped marble and made war. We Etruscans preferred to eat, drink, and love. And we loved where we lived. We never saw a need to conquer, to enslave. We love our freedom, and respect the freedom of others. No empires, thank you."

Until she was ten, her neighborhood was her world. In her parish—there were twelve churches in the town of six thousand people, looking after each parishioner's body and soul—a mob of fifty or so children ebbed and flowed in the streets, climbed the long-stepped alleyways up to the fortress, down to the spring, into Piazza Padella, or into someone's little garden terraced into the hillside behind a narrow house.

Montalcino is a medieval town of *"pieni e vuoti,"* full and empty—meaning behind each row of stone houses lining the narrow streets shoulder-to-shoulder, there is a strip of empty land giving each house its own little garden. And each little garden brims with the stuff of life: vegetables, grape vines, olives, and under the arches chickens in a coop.

When Grazietta was little, there were five butchers and six bakers in the town, two pharmacies, and a greengrocer, two doctors, a veterinarian, assorted farmers, craftsmen, lawyers, accountants, and woodcutters who sometimes stayed away in the gullies and hills for weeks. They all lived together and mingled in the town. A banker's *palazzo* was next to the cobbler, who lived an austere life, and the lawyer lived in a *palazzo* with a bridge, while beside him lived a collier with six barefooted children.

In the summer the townspeople migrated outside the town walls and up the hill of the *pineta*, a vast grove of pines where the ground was cool from the shade and the breeze from the sea blew in every day. They brought tables and chairs, and things to cook and wine. Everyone came; there was no rank or class. On those warm summer evenings they ate and drank in the *pineta* and talked as if they hadn't gossiped enough in town, then someone would begin to play an accordion or mandolin, or saxophone or guitar—all the town's craftsmen played in the town band—and they played and people danced until their houses in town cooled down enough to sleep in.

The township looked after the kids all summer long with games and outings, while the church ran summer camps at La Velona, an enchanted-looking castle on a lonely hill below the great volcano. From here there were hikes into the wild woods, or to the river, or to the hot-springs where ninety-degree water cascaded from the rocks into natural pools. There were families of *contadini* living in the castle and working the land, and, when needed, the kids would go in the fields and vineyards to lend a hand.

In the winters there were the *circoli*, big halls owned by each political party where kids could play and scream to their hearts' delight. And all year long, starting at dusk, when the sounds of mules' shoes clattered homeward on the stones, the whole town would emerge for the evening *passeggiata*, gathering in the *piazza*s and flowing through the streets, to meet and mingle and exchange the latest news or gossip with those you had somehow missed on your errands during the day.

And every week the theater featuring troupes of traveling actors was full to the rafters. There is a magnificent theater in the center of town, a scaled-down version of La Scala with a good, deep stage and three tiers of private booths with padded velvet armrests that rise toward a great fresco of a sky.

It was built a couple of centuries ago by the forty wealthiest families in the town, who then got to sit in their private balconies while the rest sat in the orchestra on benches, paying next to nothing or for free.

There were also films in the old cloister, or, in summer, the courtyard of the *fortezza*. And you could roam the streets on the darkest night without a care, because you knew exactly who'd come out each door.

And you also knew what went on behind those doors, not just from the tone of voices that ricocheted in the narrow streets when the windows were wide open from the spring into the fall—when you could tell who loved who, whose child got bad grades in school, and whose family was lacking in funds or food or care—but also through the actions of friends and neighbors. As word spread through the parish, the parish came to help. And they did so with as little fanfare as they could, sometimes just inviting a poor student to do homework with a good one, or stopping by to lend a helping hand, or creating work that hadn't needed doing just to preserve the head of the family's pride. And when small gestures weren't enough and plain money was required, the parish would discretely, through the parish priest, provide.

One winter Grazietta's family fell on hard times. The sale of bricks that her father made had suddenly slowed. Voices were tense. Meat grew scarce on the table. The father seemed to talk less every night. The next week the parish priest found Grazietta on the way home from school. He fell in step and chatted. Then up the steps of the road when he was sure no one was looking he pulled form his sleeve a stuffed envelope. "Give this to your father please," he said, "when no one else is there." He said no more, turned and strode away.

13

2 ~ QUALITY OF LIFE

When I mention Tuscany to outsiders, the usual response is a wistful sigh. And when I add sheepishly that we live out in the hills with vineyards and olives, the common rejoinder is, "You're living my dream."

What they seem to be talking about is the quality of life: the pace, the peace, the physical beauty, the social togetherness, and, of course, the food and wine. And just as Tuscan food and wine is rooted in myriad things beyond the kitchen and cellar, so the quality of life is a vast conglomeration of daily details, each of which must be of quality for all of it to work.

Time

Perhaps the most instantly impressive thing about Tuscany is the leisurely pace at which life is not just lived, but thoroughly enjoyed. We had a dear friend Nebbia, a *trovaroba*—

literally a "finder of things"—from the town of Castelmuzio. He was a remarkably talented sitter, was one of the sweetest wits of all time and loved to massacre old proverbs. He used one as the slogan of his life: "Never put off 'til tomorrow what you can put off 'til the day after."

Another friend, Bill Thompson, recounted the lesson he learned twenty years ago when he first arrived from England with ten words of Italian and a degree in agricultural economics. He began working on an estate with a single worker, Carlo, who was then 65 years old with gapped teeth that seemed to interlock. They began one day by hoeing around ancient olives using hoes designed in medieval times. Bill was young and fit, so he worked with great fervor, leaving a circular carpet of fresh earth around each tree, then moving anxiously and quickly to the next. For a while Carlo, humming happily, working at a comfortable pace, glancing over now and then, but after an hour, with Bill pouring sweat, Carlo came and took him gently by the arm. "*Fermo,*" he said. Stop. He took the hoe and, pointing to the next tree to be hoed, said, "After this one there is that one, and after that one the next." And pointing beyond to the woods, he said, "And then many more." Then he went back to his tree and calmly hoed away.

Bill was dumbfounded. He watched Carlo for a moment, then the revelation hit him: "If I can enjoy *this* tree, I've bloody got it made."

Tuscans do.

Which is why when you stop any stranger, he will

almost always look at you with pleasant anticipation, not because on your anxious face there is written something intriguing or wise, but because he has learned from experience—centuries of it, so that it's now in his genes—that each moment, given half a chance, can be the best.

That is why few Tuscans will skip their five-course lunch, because his love of life dictates that every meal should be as good as every other.

Quality of Things

Perhaps part of a Tuscan's calm comes from the ancient hamlets and towns around him, where houses, churches, and art have stood firm for centuries; and from a countryside that, for the most part, has changed little over time. There are olive groves whose trees are hundreds of years old, and vineyards that have been vineyards since Etruscan times.

History, stretching so effortlessly back, can lull you into a peaceful reverie, in the tranquilizing knowledge that so much has come before you and so much more will come after you are gone. Your efforts, big or small, will fit in with all the rest; perhaps you can add a few stones, a wall, maybe a room, or maybe a bench in the canyon by the brook so you can watch the water spume over the rocks, and hear it rumble as it rushes to the sea. Then again, if you do nothing all your life but look after your family, that's all right too, there's no need to do more.

It is this looking both back and ahead that fills you

with but a single obligation, that whatever you do, it better be your best, because if it is, it will remain for a long time. So when you build your house, it's natural to use the best material—stone for walls, clay roof tiles, copper for gutter pipes. And when a store is built, whether for a butcher or a pharmacist, its marble floors and counters are done not for show but to last your lifetime and your children's and your children's children's. And even your windows, doors, and taps are chosen with great care, because if they break and need replacement, well, that's a waste of life.

Tuscans strive for quality even in daily items. Clothes, furniture, appliances, cars, are all bought to last. Whereas North Americans tend to trade in their cars every three years, new cars around us—an affluent valley—seem to be kept about three times longer.

With my love for sailing I often visit Tuscan marinas. My first visit left me almost speechless. There were teak-decked wharves with stainless steel hardware, boxes, and railings, guaranteeing a long life for everything in sight. And in the old hill towns, where an epidemic of putting asphalt over old stone streets spread for a few years, the new surfaces being laid are all great slabs of stone. If the first stone layers lasted a thousand years, these should do at least the same.

The Towns

The first thing to strike one about Tuscan towns is their

silence. Whether small like Pienza or medium-sized like Siena, the most noteworthy thing is the absence of cars. And so it should be. The towns were designed for people, and cars were tried for a few years but their noise, their pollution, and their visual ugliness tore at the ancient fabric of Tuscan life, so little by little they were pushed to the peripheries. The streets came alive again, re-conquered by people. The bars and restaurants put tables and umbrellas where cars once roared, kids played ball in the streets again, and neighbors stopped and chatted on their daily errands or their evening *passeggiata*.

And on hot summer nights and the balmy ones of autumn, the tables outside flicker with candlelight, not just at restaurants, cafes, and bars, but in front of family houses, where tables are brought down into the street and set for dinner among neighbors and friends.

Within the towns, *le contrade*, the neighborhoods, through traditions as well as festivities create a sense of localized patriotism, a sense of civic pride which give one an even greater sense of belonging. In places like Siena, not only is each *contrada* fiercely competitive with the next, but just as fiercely each looks after its own. All of life's great events—births, deaths, marriages, and even wine and food festivals—are celebrated within the *contrada*. If a marriage takes place between two *contrada*s and the bride moves into the house of the groom, it is traditional to bring a patch of dirt from the bride's *contrada* and put it under the delivery bed, so the child would be born on its own soil.

Siena's municipal hall has a delicate tower that surveys the countryside. It is at the base of one of man's most beautiful creations: the fan-shaped, sloping *campo*, paved with brick in elegant patterns and surrounded by noble *palazzi* and topped by a marble fountain. This is where, each summer, enormous quantities of dirt are brought in to create, around the rim of the *campo*, a race track for horses for the Palio, the festive contest among the seventeen *contrade*. For days on end, parades in colorful 16th-century costumes and warm-up races with all their excitement fill the city. During those days, Siena lives as one. This cohesion lasts through the year. And if Tuscans take enormous pride in their land, the Sienese have it in aces. The municipal hall fresco, under which the city fathers work, is titled "Good Government, Bad Government," and it may just explain why Tuscan towns function so well for all. It shows a tranquil and harmonious life lived when governed by the first, and the decay and suffering brought on by the second. The written narrative describes bad government as "Concerned with protecting its own interest rather than the common good."

It is a fresco every Tuscan schoolchild knows by heart.

Health

Much has been written about the Mediterranean diet, not just its simplicity and boundless fresh flavors but also its positive influence on health. Using olive oil in copious quantities as its only fat, and rich in vegetables, bread, legumes, fruit, and pasta, with chicken and fish and only occasional red meat, it has been credited with aiding a long and healthy life.

Yet the food alone is not enough to account for Tuscans living into an active old age. Every country house and nearly every house in town has a large food garden. Tuscans without outdoor space often find a plot of land just outside of town, where they grow lush miracles with only a spade and a hoe. Not only does a home garden keep you eating well and fit, but it's the rest of daily life in both town and country that contributes to the healthy existence.

The exclusion of cars from towns has put the pleasure back in walking, and it's not unusual to see octogenarians merrily packing their daily shopping—most things are bought fresh each day—up the steepest streets of medieval towns.

The obsession with doing it yourself keeps the men active well after they have officially retired from jobs, and the women, whose houses are truly their castles, are kept in constant motion maintaining their domain. I honestly can't remember entering a Tuscan house and finding the lady of the house sitting watching television; they are endlessly and productively busy. As Nebbia, the eternal bachelor, upon passing a door wherein the mistress of the house was sweeping up a storm, quietly quipped, "Men make houses; but women," he sighed, "make me very nervous." When I asked some of the ladies if instead of working around the house they would prefer a career in town, the majority looked at me as if I had lost my mind. I must admit that working at home among family and friends, making unforgettable meals and looking after your own, really does sound better than most outside jobs.

~

Then there is the sense of security and tranquility instilled by Italy's medical system. Not only is all medical care free, precluding all anxiety about paying for medical insurance or going without and risking a financial collapse in case of serious illness, but there are two other aspects of the system that allow Tuscans to go through illnesses with great dignity and calm. First is the primary care. In towns and in the country there are district doctors. Since the community is spread out—including not just Montalcino but also hamlets like Sant'Angelo and Camigliano—instead of having those feeling ill travel a great distance, Dr. Talenti sets up shop, in the form of a tiny but efficient dispensary, in each hamlet three times a week.

Even more accommodating than these facilities are his house calls—which can be considered a near-miracle in modern times. For the bed-ridden, even if it's only the flu, Dr. Talenti will drive the country roads and arrive with his irrepressible good cheer to set things right again. And it's not only his presence that sets your mind at ease, but the mere knowledge that he will come when needed leaves a reassuring tranquility somewhere in your mind.

21

Another old tradition has also been kept alive. In case of hospitalization, custom has it that one family member remains in the sick room through the stay. For those staying overnight, a bed is often provided. I don't think I need to describe how reassuring it must be, especially for the very young or very old, to have present someone dear to you when you most need them.

Food

Perhaps nothing speaks of the good life as eloquently as Tuscan food. And its quality is not limited only to what's homegrown; one needs only to look at the average bakery, butcher, or even supermarket to realize that quality food is insisted on by all.

Of course there is a price to pay—free-range, hormone-free chickens and calves that take twice as long to grow, consuming twice the feed and labor, will of course cost more. And hand-baked bread that's crisp and fresh each day has a cost far beyond its industrial mate. But all this quality that we pay for, that we come in contact with each day, has its payback. When we are given the best bread one can make, or the best *prosciutto* or the tastiest, ripest fruit and vegetables, we feel good, feel worthy, feel that someone has bothered to care about what we eat. In turn, whatever we do, we do our best, and that is bound to somehow end up on the butcher's or baker's table.

When I'm treated like a king in a simple *trattoria*—and

I don't mean fawning service, I mean good, honest food prepared with those two magic ingredients "love" and "care"— then I will return to work that afternoon and will, in all likelihood, put that same love and care into whatever I do. And so it goes. Care begets care, quality begets quality, until it ends up the very foundation of a culture, where people don't do shoddy work because they don't know how. And when quality so permeates a culture, its pursuit becomes reflexive, becomes a way of living that results in an irreplaceable quality of life.

3 ~ WHERE HAVE ALL OUR NEIGHBORS GONE?

*T*uscans cling to family as tenaciously as any people in the world. Many homes house three or four generations, kids often end up in the family business, and not only does the extended family spend all festivities together, but on most Sundays cousins, uncles, nephews and grandmas descend on one another, and of course if a hand is needed, whether in sickness or in health, a relative pops up instantly to provide. And yet as precious as those relatives are, there is an old Tuscan saying that's still sacred today: A good neighbor is worth a dozen relatives.

Not long ago in both Europe and North America, "neighbor" and "neighborhood" were very special words. The neighborhood was the "countryside" of our home, where we knew people, where we felt safe, where we felt we belonged. It was where children were shoved out the door each morning and told to go play and be back for lunch. Where they went and what they did was seldom asked; the neighbors and the neighborhood looked after them all. And it wasn't just a question of looking out for the Boogey man; the neighbors and the neighborhood actually brought you up. Being reprimanded by a neighbor for bad behavior was as accepted *and* expected as a helping hand—being involved was more than the neighbor's right; it seemed, by and large, to be his obligation. That was how kids learned to be social, that's where their actions were followed by instant reactions, where they received judgments untainted by either the affection—or lack of it—of their family. If a child was spoiled at home, the neighborhood corrected that; if his family ignored him, the neighbors filled the void. Of course it wasn't all roses; at times angry words flew, and at others, flower pots, but through the tiny daily interactions, you learned what punishments and what rewards humanity had in store. From constantly interacting with neighbors old and young, you became "streetwise," meaning you learned how to navigate through life.

While there were no official neighborhood services, when the need arose, the neighbors would be there. Whether it was moving a couch, fixing the car, lending a cup of sugar or even money, picking up something from the store, or babysitting cats or children or even cooking for the sick, a helping neighborly hand was just a knock away. In a recent BBC interview during a life-threatening blizzard that swept the British Isles, the head of London's social services was concerned about the elderly who lived alone getting through the storm. He said the best protection was "an old-fashioned remedy" of checking in on neighbors to see if they were well, or if a nasty draft could be fixed, or just to make sure their heater was working. And he added, nostalgically, "it's what we used to call neighborliness." Something we seem to have forgotten along the way.

~

In the Tuscan countryside, "neighborliness" is still carried to extremes. When you need a hand with anything at all you call a neighbor; when much of one thing ripens in your garden or orchard your neighbor receives a full basket; when a hunter has good luck the neighbors share the feast; baked goods often flow freely back and forth—and when a neighbor is sick, or needs a field plowed or just firewood, you are there to help. Even though Dr. Talenti still makes his reassuring house calls, when medication is needed or in dire cases injections need be given, the most experienced of the neighbors comes to give it. When Candace, my nearest and dearest, had bronchial pneumonia, our next-door neighbor Marina walked the quarter mile, twice daily, from her house beside the church, to administer antibiotic injections, which—along with her garlic-and-basil-filled *ragu*—saved Candace's life.

Yet as important as these physical gestures are, perhaps even more so is the emotional reassurance of being surrounded by people who care. You become not just satisfied and content with what you have, but through that, more relaxed, more open. You become that worn but befitting term: "happy."

Each time I return to Italy, I exhale a deep sigh; then, driving along the sea through the hills, I calm some more, but when I see the stone church steeple and turn onto the dirt road a mile from our house, and drive by Bartolommei's, then Castelli's, then Marina's little place, my heart feels good; I'm in my neighborhood. I'm home.

Just how happy our neighbors make us, how much happiness we derive or "catch" from those close to us, was actually quantified in an intriguing study led by the Harvard Medical School. The questionnaire asked five thousand adults to identify relatives, close friends, place of residence, and place of work. They were asked whether they enjoyed life, felt hopeful about the future, were happy, and felt they were just as good as other people. The researchers followed up with the participants every two to four years. The results were stunning. Strangely enough, the "happiness" of a coworker had no effect at all—possibly due to competition in the workplace, or even a case of *schadenfreude*. On the other hand, live-in partners who became happy increased the likelihood of their partner being happy by 8%. Very similar effects were found for siblings living close by at 14%, but what was most astounding was the happiness effect of neighbors: it weighed in at a whopping 34%. The only thing that surpassed it was the happiness of a friend living less than a mile away.

The leader of the study, Professor Nicholas Christakis, concluded that "people are embedded in social networks and that health and well-being of one person affects the health and well-being of others."

Yet how little time and effort do we spend cultivating the friendship of our neighbor? What happened to that time not so long ago when all of us knew everyone up and down the block? Is it that we no longer have the time? Or is it just easier to e-mail someone a thousand miles away; quicker, less demanding of our involvement, investment, and care? Or is it perhaps the fault of our new, mass-produced neighborhoods, without sidewalks to encourage strolling and visiting? Or is it because we lost that most sociable of North American inventions, the front porch?

When I was growing up in Vancouver, the front porch was a socializing wonder: if you sat there long enough you could talk to the whole world. The neighbors drifted by and leaned on the fence and chatted, or came and plopped down in a chair and talked, and Ernie Flint came to bum a cigarette, and John Hardy's sister sat on the steps and did her nails, and you listened to Eddy gripe about his chickens, or to the baker moan about his never-silent wife, or you complained to Mom about weird ol' Mrs. Kindler, who filled up six blackboards in biology and made you copy down every bloody word. Or you could just sit and watch the girls walk or the kids play, or park Granny in her rocking chair.

But times have changed a lot in thirty years. Granny is off in some distant "home," the kids are getting ulcers at the ball park, Mom's at work, the friends are busy washing down the yacht, and the neighbor waves as he rushes from car to house calling out "Hi there," because he doesn't know your name. And the front porches are gone, replaced by forbidding three-car garages.

The death of the neighborhood didn't happen overnight; it snuck up slowly, a thoughtlessness here, a tiny neglect there, a bit too much ambition, a little too much greed. It snuck up on us slowly like the greenhouse effect, the Wall Street madness, the anxiety-riddled society we've become. And what of the future? How much will things change now that our lives are so frantic that we have less time to care, less time to reflect? And no Granny on the front porch to remind us of simpler times, better days.

~

So, where have all the neighbors gone? Not just in America but in Europe, in the country? And what have we found to replace the "happiness" and "well-being" that the Harvard Study found they provided? If the experience of two hamlets, one in Tuscany and the other in the Dolomites of Northern Italy, is typical, then the answer is, not much.

From the ridge outside the medieval hill-town of Montepulciano where the Tuscan hamlet lies, there is a breathtaking view of the town's walls and steeples rising against the sky. A dirt road on that ridge winds across the valley, dotted every few hundred yards by a stone house. The land here is unforgiving clay, which can be worked at only the right moistness—too dry and it is brick-hard; too wet and it's a swamp.

Grains grow well here, as do heat-loving olives, and the vineyards produce an austere, now world-famous wine called Vino Nobile di Montepulciano. But a few decades ago the wine was not so famous, and the families working the land—the Paoluccis, the Bazzottis, and the Scaccini twins down the hill—just eked out a living and no more. Some were in *mezzadria*—meaning they worked the land for a half share of the crops, while the other half went to the owner of the house and land—others were their own masters and earned a hard but good life from the clay. And although each house and tract of land belonged to different owners, the families often worked together as if they were one.

Harvesting the wheat began at one house, and when the thrashing was done and the sacks full, no matter what time of day or night, everyone settled down under the arbors in the warm June air for an enormous feast and wine. Afterwards, out came the accordions and songs and, with all fatigue forgotten, they began to dance. With bellies full and cheeks aglow, they would get a few hours' sleep, then, at first light, move on to harvest at the next farm. There was but one old wooden thrasher in the valley, and at harvest time it worked almost round the clock. So on it went: harvest/feast, harvest/feast, until all the valley's grain was safely in the sacks. The *vendemmia*, the grape harvest, was much the same, only the feasts were longer.

The annual pig killing, with the preparation of *prosciutto*s, sausages, bacon, and salamis was a two-day affair at each house with the neighbors chipping in.

During the rest of the year, the helping hand and festive spirit stayed. Roads were fixed together, machines were cursed together, wood cutting shared, and cattle taken to pasture in joint herds. And since Tuscan meals—whether handmade pastas, or slowly simmering sauces, or wood-oven-roasted partridges or Guinea hens—take a long time to prepare, it was traditional that only one house cooked each day. The neighbors, all three generations of them, often including bachelor uncles and "old maid" sisters, joined in on the dinners. The men spent the rest of the evening on eternal card games, the women sewed and knitted, and the kids played tirelessly in and around the house.

When Paolucci recounted this to me, I told him how envious I was for having missed those years. His eyes smiled, he the turned wistful and said, *"Madonna, quelli erano tempi veri"*—Virgin Mary, those were real times.

Then I told him how great it was to still have a neighbor like him who you can count on through thick and thin. He looked at me and said gently, "It's nice to be needed."

But things changed three decades ago along the dirt road in the valley. The wine gained world fame, tourists came, restaurants and *enotecas* mushroomed, and there were good part-time jobs to be had, so the families started bringing in extra cash. Montepulciano got wealthy. And the families, with their new-found wealth, spent more and more time shopping: for cars, new tractors, televisions. They bought speedy gas-powered hay-cutters instead of hand-held scythes and refrigerators that could hold a week's pre-cooked meals so no one had to prepare dinner every night. There was much less need for a neighbor's helping hand, hence many fewer occasions for a neighbor to be needed.

~

In the craggy mountains of the Dolomites, an isolated hamlet just below the tree line suffered a similar fate.

La Pieve is at the end of a tortuous road etched into cliffs above a roaring torrent. Until a few decades ago there was no safe road, only a winding trail that the mountain people had used for centuries. Pink-rocked peaks tower around the town, and below the peaks are thick forests and steep pastures where cowbells break the silence. This is south Tyrol: the houses are ancient, built of *larice*, a wood that dries hard and resists rot. Geraniums in flower boxes cascade below the windows. Pieve has a hotel built in the thirteen-hundreds where they serve the world's best handmade ravioli—the pasta so thin you can see right through it—and a roast pig's shank that will live forever in your memory. There's a church from some century or other with a spire steeper than the mountains, and a couple dozen houses that look across the valley to the peaks beyond. A thousand feet above the town is the hamlet of Las Casas, where the view is so dramatic it's hard to close your eyes.

A rough track leads to the hamlet from the road. On a bit of flatland huddle the hamlet's three houses, three ancient wooden barns, a stout stone shed with a small loft above, and a tiny chapel with three worn pinewood benches. Below the houses rushes a stream, and beside it stands a flour mill firm and solid, all of wood—the walls, the shoots, the waterwheel, and even the great cog wheels that helped to turn the stones. Not long ago the three houses—none related—lived like one big family.

We rented an attic in one of the houses for a year. In the house lived two brothers in their forties, neither ever married; next door was a couple and their adult son; and in the third, two elderly spinsters and their aging bachelor brother with a meticulous mustache.

The steep slopes around the hamlet are covered by flowering hay in spring, in the winter by thick snow. The slopes were worked by hand, manure pitch-forked, the hay scythed, and the soil that the rains washed down, hauled to the top of the fields again. Each house had its own cows, but shared in carting the big tins of milk and in taking the cows to alpine pastures above the tree line in late spring, then herding them home together when the first snowflakes came on the hard wind from the north.

Odd chores were divided in the hamlet. Joseph, one of the brothers, ran a one-man sawmill; the adult son of the house next door did carpentry and cabinets; Tony, Joseph's brother, tended an enormous vegetable garden; one of the sisters looked after the chickens; the couple and the old brother tended the milk cows in the barn; and the other sister cooked with a wild passion. They ate together, prayed in the chapel together, and played music together: accordion, clarinet, and horn. Until the money.

Nearby, Kron Plaz is a strangely rounded mountain with gentle sides among peaks and broken crags. It's 7,500 feet high, with some of the finest alpine pastures in the range. In winter, snow piles deep on it and you can ski in any direction, a 5,000-foot drop to the valley far below. The world found out, and it built lifts, hotels, and shops. Tourists came. The people of the hamlet began working part time for good pay on the lifts and in restaurants, and the ties that held them so close through the years began to fray. They began to bicker—about who parked whose car on the edge of whose field, who built a fence that cut the corner of whose land, who owed who how much for a borrowed piece of board, or whose TV was playing much too loud. They stopped working together and eating together, and even stopped going together to the chapel.

And now when they pass each other, as they often must, their speech is strained, or sometimes they don't speak at all. And there's no sound of clarinet or accordion or horn in the cold, and long, and star-filled winter night.

~

And apart from some household appliances and cars, what have the people of Las Casas really gained? As far as I can tell, nothing but loneliness, with some sadness and bitterness stirred in now and then. Individually they're still wonderful people, warm, lively, full of vigor—the old sisters still walk a mile down a path to Pieve to buy their groceries, then walk the mile back all uphill loaded down with bags—and were generous to us with gifts of firewood and *porcini* and a bottle of still-warm milk on our doorstep every morning. And they tell us in a flat voice that they know what they have lost: closeness, contentment, daily entertainment, a sense of being appreciated for your work or your jokes or your prowess on the mountain, whether it's finding mushrooms or climbing forbidding peaks or running the little mill that still stands beside the stream. And even though they seem to know what they have lost, somehow they just don't know how to get it back again.

~

What, you may ask, has the social breakdown of two isolated hamlets to do with modern life? What does it have to do with the rest of us? Well, it seems to me, everything. If people who had shared so much can so easily drift apart, can be driven apart by such modest bits of wealth, just think how loose the ties have become in our own neighborhoods.

And just as the people of Las Casas have driven themselves into exile in their houses, so, in cities and in suburbs, have we done to ourselves. We live in fabulous McMansions or lavish apartments filled with the latest gadgets that serve and entertain, but in terms of a real society, of true neighbors and friends, with whom we share our daily lives, we simply are no more. We live, by and large, socially shipwrecked. And without friends, our meals have lost a little flavor, and the wine seems somehow to have gone a little flat. And there is a kind of sadness to drinking alone; somewhat akin to dancing solo in the dark.

And just as bad, if not worse: when pleasure or help no longer comes from neighbors, when all services and entertainment need be paid for every time, then no wonder when our incomes fall we feel such devastation. Our life comes to a standstill without the ability to spend. No wonder we panic when the world affects our pockets: in a pay-for-each-breath culture our pocket *is* our life.

When I asked Paolucci how his life changed during the recession of the oil crises of the seventies, he shrugged his shoulders. "There was one thing," he said. "Instead of the tractor, I used the donkey to pull carts of firewood from the creek. And you know what? It saved time. When I whistled, the donkey came. That stupid tractor just sits there until I go and get it."

4 ～ SUNDAY

*N*ot so long ago, we had a sensible society that resembled that of Tuscany in a most important aspect: we thrived on each other's company. But we have changed in one generation to a people thrilled, to the point of being mesmerized, by objects—so much so that the former president of the United States no longer referred to his co-nationals as "Fellow Americans" or "Citizens" or even "Countrymen," but simply—and unapologetically—as "the consumer." To appreciate what happened, perhaps it's enough to look at Sundays.

Whoever invented Sunday was a genius, ranking right up there with the inventor of the sofa. We seem to be an easygoing race that will put up with the dullest routine so long as we get our regular breaks: we turn morose if we don't get eight hours' sleep and become homicidal when deprived of our morning coffee. Mr. Sunday knew that. So he stirred in a day of rest every seven days, not only to give our worn muscles an intermission but also so our brains could switch from the same old tracks. He knew that fresh thoughts and conversations invigorate our minds just as much as a good massage invigorates our bodies.

Just a few decades ago our Sundays were about people. I used to wake up when Tommy Flint next door started yelling at the short fat dog he was trying to turn into Rin Tin Tin. But the fat dog didn't get fat by being stupid. When Tommy leapt over the fence and ordered him to follow, Fat Dog amicably ambled to a post, sniffed, then had himself a comfy little pee. That's when Tommy went ballistic and shook me from my dreams. Later his dad Ernie would shuffle over in his worn-toed slippers, bum a cigarette from my mom, set himself down at the kitchen table, and nibble what was left of breakfast while discussing with my dad his garden or the world while my mom began cooking one of her enormous Sunday meals.

Ours was a modest, working class Vancouver neighborhood with narrow lots, small gardens, four-room houses, and some trees to shade the sidewalks. Sunday mornings the streets were peaceful and empty. Only chubby Eddy Emanoff would creak by on his old bike and, like some bemused Paul Revere, try to rouse the neighborhood to a ballgame at the schoolyard. Not a soul ever showed up before lunch. Eddy knew that, but he liked to creak about on that bike anyway, up the street and down the back lane only to end up lying on our lawn trying to talk me into trading my Mickey Mantle card for some weird guy called Turk Lown.

After a Hungarian lunch of two-hour-simmered chicken soup, roast meats with paprika and sour cream sauces, a cucumber salad, and enough buttery, flakey, fresh-baked pastries to feed an army, I was out the door with my glove, running for the field with my mother shouting, "Be careful yourself! What happen if you die?"

Then we played ball. We had no teams, no coaches, no uniforms, no bases, only an old chipped bat and a few gloves that we shared, and the school yard was no well-manicured diamond but an old soccer field of dusty weeds and gravel. The gravel gave you strange bounces in the gut and privates but you got used to that—what irked you every time was that short, right-field fence a hundred and fifty feet away. And Al Crowder. The bastard hit left handed. Squinty little eyes, cigarette dangling from his mouth, and bang—a home run. John Hardy would climb the fence when Crowder came to bat, but bloody Crowder never hit right at him, so Hardy would end up talking to Mrs. Thompson working her vegetable garden in her floppy hat.

Anyway, we picked teams by sticking our feet in a circle and someone reeling off "Engine, engine number nine going down Chicago line," then we'd yell and fight who got to play where. Then we'd settle down and play serious ball, until Eddy Emanoff hit one of his hard grounders to the fence and rounded first base chuckling and puffing, but second base was a bit uphill and Eddy never made it because Jerry Allye would jump him, drag him down, and beat him with his glove while Eddy died laughing. Some of us would wander off during the game and others wander in; sometimes

<label>39</label>

parents stopped by to watch and some even stayed to play, Ernie Flint running the bases in his worn-toed slippers.

The best part was John Hardy's sister. She was a bit older, soft and round, and loved to play but was growing her nails so she refused to wear a glove. She held it and just threw it at grounders. And to catch pop flies—we loved pop flies—she'd raise the hem of her shirt and hold it out like a net. Then any guy near her knelt to tie his laces. When the sun got so low it shone in our eyes, we went home. One day the fog rolled in and we snuck off and left Hardy sitting on the fence.

On too-hot summer Sundays we went fishing. We would get in my family's twenty-horsepower Austin that was built like a tank and also crawled like one, and we'd putt-putt out to this creek a half-hour from the house, grownups with kids, grownups without kids, kids without grownups, nobody really cared. It was a lousy place to fish. You might hook a few fat catfish or a carp, but the hayfields were a nice place to lie, or you could kick a ball around down on the bank, and the willows gave you shade, and in a bend the water was deep and the mud on the bottom squished between your toes. Then we'd build a fire and make a stew from everybody's fish in a big pot.

A few times a year we went to search for gold. There was a gold rush in the canyon of the Fraser River a century ago, and a friend's great uncle was said to have buried five bags of gold he had panned below a raging cataract called Hell's Gate.

So a flock of us would descend among the rocks, trying to make sense of a map someone had drawn, and we'd yell and shout because the cataract roared so loud, then we'd move a few stones and pick at a bit of dirt before roasting sausages and drinking lots of homemade wine while we discussed where the gold could be or just lay around and talked. We seemed to talk a lot on all those Sundays.

But that was years ago.

I visited friends in Florida last spring. Paradise. Palm trees, canals, bougainvilleas, gardenias, majestic white egrets standing in the shoals. I tried to sleep in on Sunday morning but jumped awake to a frightening sound like an F15 landing on the roof. It was a leaf blower. Behind a weed eater. On the canal, jet skis screamed and cigarette boats roared. On the street, kids on dirt bikes without mufflers leapt over curved ramps, and on almost every perfect lawn, on a mower the size of our Austin, were large and grumpy men crouched like warriors riding tanks to war. By ten it was rush hour. Great campers and SUVs stacked to the roof with gear headed to the beach a ten minute walk away. There was a bottleneck at the mall; it hadn't yet opened but the entrance to the parking lot was jammed. On Sunday. Our sacred day of rest.

I headed down to the beach on foot—not easy without sidewalks—using the road or people's lawns, dodging cars and mowers. At the mall I asked one of the waiting crowd at the still-locked doors if there was a special sale. There wasn't. This was just an ordinary Sunday. Was anyone left at home for that special Sunday meal?

That afternoon I stopped to watch a ballgame of kids as young as Hardy when he sat on the fence. My God, what a ballpark! A real diamond: a pitcher's mound, Astroturf infield, raked sand between bases, real bases, dugouts, benches, uniforms, spikes, kids with their own gloves and kid gloves for batting and bats. Man, did they have bats, racks of aluminum bats. Enough to melt down and build a 747.

And yet, awash in material splendor, everyone was as solemn as if someone had just died. Anxious parents loudly urged victory, agitated kids yelled tired slogans, and, growing frustrated, threw their gloves in anger. The worst was when the kids in the field came to bat. The lip-biting coach called them into a huddle, hectored them to "stay aggressive, give 'em hell, shake 'em up, go in for the kill!" because they had those guys "scared now," they had them "on the run."

What was this? War? Or just kids playing ball? Couldn't they wait until they grew up to have a bad time? Where was chubby Eddy Emanoff? Where was John Hardy's sister? Where was Ernie Flint in his worn-toed slippers? Maybe I'm raving; maybe the years are coloring my youth. But I don't think so. I remember a lot of bad, but not on Sundays.

Then you may rightly ask what on earth has a ballgame got to do with our endangered society? Well, it seems to me, everything. Not only was the ball game an environmental disaster with the enormous quantity of energy consumed and pollution emitted to fabricate all those bats, uniforms, bleachers, and all, but what was sad, what broke the heart, was that despite the gear, the material splendor, there wasn't a kid out there having any fun. Sure they played well, snapped a throw, showed hustle, but where was the joy? The freedom? The laughter? Where was that burst of irrepressible urge that made Dave Dowset chase a fly ball and, after making the catch, keep running through the gate and vanish around a corner, leaving us all standing there without a ball, only to return from the fruit stand with a bag of cherries?

We shared those cherries just as we shared the gloves. That's why we came. Not just to hit home runs or beat the other guy—we played as hard as we could, we really tried—but there was more. We came to be together. To be friends.

And it didn't matter whose team you played on, or who hit best or who caught best; it didn't matter how old you were, or if you were—God forbid—a girl, and it didn't even matter if you were fat and slow. It would have been unthinkable to play a game without Eddy; the day would have been sad without his laughter.

So we played together, and sat around together, and learned to get along without parents, without coaches, on our own. We learned how to make each other laugh, and what would make us cry, and learned that if something hurt one of us it would somehow hurt us all. And I learned that you can use the same scruffy ball and chipped bat for years and still be happy, that you can have as much fun in old sneakers as in spikes, and that all the gear in the world could never be worth one of my mother's enormous, Sunday meals.

Organized to Death

When I played backup quarterback in my high school senior year, I lugged my gear around with boundless pride. I know being part of that team emboldened my timid heart, and I'm sure we had some good times and shared struggles in mud and snow, but what took the joy out of it was that it was just an extension of the long, long hours of school. It was organized. Supervised. You were told what to do. You had to learn rigid plays with a long list of rigid numbers. If you didn't, the coach had a fit. Creativity and spontaneity were a last resort. It took a broken play before you could finally invent, feel independent, have a bit of fun.

I was on the soccer team a couple of years before that. Being Hungarian I had played soccer in the cradle. When I was five, we played soccer in the streets, with no real ball but one that we made by stuffing newspapers into a sock and then twisting the sock and sewing it tight. With that much practice—in Hungary ball handling was considered art—I was the most experienced on that team in Canada, adept at dribbling and faking with my feet. Yet halfway through the first game the coach pulled me off, grumbling, "We don't need fancy footwork."

In Tuscany, as in most parts of the world, you play soccer where you can: in the church yard, the *piazza*, the post office parking lot, under the arches of the Uffizzi, in the flatter part of the Il Campo in Siena. No uniforms, no coaches, no organization. Now I know many of you will say organized sports teach discipline, but don't we have enough discipline already? And if you say organized sports teach important skills, yes, but that's only vital for small dogs in the circus who jump and twist through rings.

And another thing. For the twenty-five kids who made that high school football team, there were many more who didn't. And so many more who never even came, too afraid or embarrassed even just to try. How did they feel? What scars were left on their frail young hearts? I know of one who was "cut" in baseball. She was one of two. And even now, thirty years later, when she talks about it, tears spring to her eyes. Then she mutters, with her teeth clenched, "the bitch."

No one would have these memories from our Sundays. In winter we played hockey on a frozen pond. One kid, Bobby Murphy, was such a hopeless skater that we used to call him "Minus." But he played anyway, not at all perplexed; flailing, stumbling, often missing passes; and of us all it was Minus Murphy who, even more then the rest, had the most exuberant, wild time of his life.

And that ragged Sunday group is forever in my memories as the solid and joyful foundation of my life—one of my recent best days was with Dave Dowset on his birthday.

The members of that football team, I don't think of at all.

～

I know I'm raising hair on the backs of necks, for we parents seem to think that organized sports are as vital as mother's milk. We should ask ourselves, why? And we should ask our children if they really like it. *Really* like it, or are they just doing it to please and humor us. So maybe that next time we drive them to a ballgame, we should just for a moment stop the car, take a breath and think again, then turn off onto some side road, find a simple school ground, and spend some precious time playing ball. With them.

In our small town here in Tuscany, there's a beautiful soccer field below the ancient fortress and a perfectly-organized team for kids. I took our son, Buster—as in "Listhen Busther" slurred by my hero, Daffy Duck—to join up when he was ten. He was a good player, kicked like a mule, scored goals from ten yards—we had played in the garden at home, blasting balls past each other at the stone wall of the house—and he didn't dislike team play and knew most of the kids, but he bristled at the long, dull drills of practice and the lengthy games during which you seldom touched the ball. After a few weeks he said one day, "Dad, can't we just play at Camigliano?"

Camigliano—population nineteen—is a hilltop hamlet at road's end, alone in a wild valley. A one-room school house still stands from long ago, with a tiny soccer field etched into the hill. The views stop your heart: vineyards, olive groves, rolling hills, a castle, a lake, two rivers—one south one west—and to the east a snow-capped old volcano. We played. The two of us. We played on the same team, running up and down, passing back and forth, and finally shooting at the goal where an unsuspecting lawn chair had been recruited to play goalie. Then we played against each other, faking and dribbling, panting as we ran our guts out, and cursed and yelled when the ball sailed over the fence, over a wall, and into a garden of *carciofi*—artichokes. While the kicker climbed the wall, we sang "*Carciofi* fields forever." We played summer and winter, a couple of times a week. That was years ago. I'm past sixty now. But when Buster comes home from college on infrequent holidays, the first chance we get we go to Camigliano. To dribble and fake and blast. And climb the bloody stone wall into the *carciofi* field.

Forever.

5 ~ WHERE WE FEEL
AT HOME

I'm not sure why a small town so predictably stirs my heart. Whether it's an Irish village with a pub on the green, a hamlet in Vermont with a white clapboard steeple, a medieval hill town of stone in Tuscany, or just a row of frail houses under mangos in the Marquesas, something in me says, "Here's a good place to live."

The first decade of my life I spent in a dreary city (Budapest), my teens in a more gardened one (Vancouver), then a year in west Los Angeles with the hubbub and excitement of studios and bright lights, yet I always felt restless. Until one day I drove down the coast, through green hills with grazing cows, and came out of the wild canyon into a town with the sparkling sea, and I thought, "Okay. I'm never leaving."

It was Laguna Beach in 1967.

Laguna was the last seaside town surrounded by a greenbelt, which gave you the sensation of a country on its own. Some people lived above the sandstone cliffs that loomed over the shore, in tiny, single-walled cottages lining narrow, shady streets with names like Bluebird Canyon Drive and Lombardy Lane, while others lived in homemade houses in the deep shadows of what was called "The Canyon."

There were a few stores across from the beach—surf shops, two bookstores, a couple selling tie dyes and trinkets from India, and a brand new library where you could rush on Tuesday morning and laugh at the cartoons of the fresh *New Yorker* for free.

But mostly there was the beach. The houses along the beach were on the bluff far above, so the strip of sand below felt like a private world. Full of people. Night and day.

It was a time when no one seemed to have much of a job, or at least not one that interfered with the vital things in life: friends, the beach, surfing. Some worked a few hours in shops, others at Albertson's supermarket; some made surfboards in the morning so they could surf all afternoon, and almost all of those in the canyon grew and smoked whatever they could find, and, when the whim hit or their pockets were empty, turned out some remarkable pieces of craft and art. The phrase "greenhouses gases" was not invented yet, but I think if you had measured the carbon footprint of that town, it would have been close to that of a Bantu village in Africa.

After a week, you knew most people at least by sight, and you were reflexively invited to cookouts on the beach, or parties in the canyon, or touch football in a field. In that

beach town, no matter how poor you were or what a hand-
built shack you lived in, or how many of you shared a tiny
flat above the bar, or if you didn't have a place to stay and had
to crash with someone, you were still embraced as a citizen of
the town.

Best of all were the weekends in the desert. Local rock
bands or musicians would start to spread the word at mid-
week about some desolate valley not far inland, and by Friday
afternoon everyone was packed and ready with a sleeping bag
or blanket; food you could buy from farm stands along the
way.

So the bands went and a few hundred of us went,
stacked five or six into Volkswagens or trucks, and nothing
was organized and everything was free, and everyone passed
around whatever they had brought, and there were bonfires,
great pots of chili and mountains of oranges and watermelon.
The moonlit desert air was sweet with curling smoke, and
dust rose from the dancing, and the music was so righteous
that the moon didn't seem to want to ever leave the sky.

And you drove back slowly Sunday, silent and exhausted but grinning, because you had just had the best time of
your life.

~

Memories of that endless summer and that easy-going small
town never left me, and I searched thereafter for a feeling like
Laguna of 1967.

That fall I went back to university in Vancouver. I

needed a place to live, but apartment rents were high and while my part-time job on a tugboat covered my tuition, to pay for rent I'd have to put in more time; I began to run out of hours in the day. I must confess that I went to university not just for education; I went to find the love of my life. Hence the quandary: if I had to spend all day in classes, then evenings on the tugs just to pay the rent, just when exactly could I hunt the lady of my dreams? In my sleep? On my coffee break? In the middle of the sea?

I realize that some will frown at a woman-chaser taking up space at a university, and I also accept that nowadays higher education is but a springboard to a lucrative career, yet back then we seemed to have a different view of life. We weren't in school for work training, or a career foundation; we weren't there to learn how to land a "steady job"—in fact, I thought we were there to learn how to live *without* one. We were there to learn about people, ourselves, and the world. What would happen after we graduated we didn't have a clue.

I suppose we had the same idea about education as a Harvard admissions committee, which decades later declared, "The aim of a liberal education is to unsettle presumptions, to defamiliarize the familiar, to reveal what is going on beneath and behind appearances, to disorient young people and to help them to find ways to reorient themselves."

Well, the disorientation worked thoroughly on me; whether I ever reoriented is still up for debate.

Anyway, I was running out of hours; something had to

go. It was the rent.

On the way home from Laguna I had stopped in Sausalito, and seen my salvation. I was staying with friends up in the hills—endless views, eucalyptus fragrance, fine house—but what grabbed my attention was Sausalito Bay, full of houseboats. They were the funkiest, handmade-est, imagination-running-wildest houseboats you could dream of. Every shape and size, built on old barges, or old tow boats, or rafts of redwood logs, or even sea plane floats. Some were leaning, some sinking, but all laden with potted flowers and colorful people. They all seemed to know each other, and help out each other, and sit around and smoke and drink beer with each other. It was Laguna Beach afloat.

When the tug I worked on idled while loading scows, I rowed along the dark Vancouver waterfront, searching every rickety marina for a barge or raft, anything that floated, upon which I could build myself a little house. And it wasn't only the cheap rent that drew me—the moorage would cost only ten dollars a month—I was charmed by the people who lived in those marinas: fishermen on old double-ended trawlers, sailors on all sorts of boats preparing to cruise the world, and even an optometrist who traveled the coast in her old motor boat, calling on native villages among the islands and the fjords. Adventurers, dreamers, people who loved the sea. And like all lovers of the sea, they loved to talk about her: the currents, the dangers, the hundreds of islands, the best anchorages, and of course their boats. And they all had the inextinguishable sparkle in their eyes of those who, besides loving the sea, were all in love with life. Years later, I found the same passion in Tuscans, but theirs was for the land. They possessed the same thrill for hunting for *porcini*, or the best month to plant garlic, or how best to prune your vines or salt down *prosciutto*, or the best way to stuff a goose with prunes, bread, and liver soaked in wine.

And the people of the sea and of the land had another thing in common: they ran their own lives. No one told them when to wake up, or what time to be where, or what to do all day. Nor did they have to fill in time 'til five o'clock, when they finally got to do something they really liked. They were free and content—but more about this later.

~

Anyway, they were all exuberant dreamers, each of them great company, who got me hooked on the sea, for life.

Then I found my dream.

It was a 24-foot-long by 12-foot-wide scow—a miniature river barge. It had been built the year before, the wood was still fresh, the deck wide and clean, just like a tiny lot waiting for a house. It had sat there over a year—the owner changed his plans and told the marina they could have it for back rent, so for $150 that floating lot was mine. God must have started with such a scow when he started building Heaven.

I started to build a cabin.

I had helped my step-dad frame up a garage and build a fence, so I knew there was nothing to it, plus I had friends

who would gladly help. The key was to keep the design simple. I did: a box. With a somewhat oversized, overhanging
lid. I'll rave about the houseboat a bit later, but let me mention an important point here: size. Leaving a bit of foredeck
and some sidedeck to work the cleats, I ended up with about
200 square feet of space to live in. Not much, I grant you, but
maybe there lies the key to a sociable neighborhood: the
smaller the place you live in, the more likely you'll get out
and socialize. Most of the houseboats in Sausalito were small
as were the cottages of Laguna Beach, as were the fishing
boats and sailboats of the marina of the scow. Perhaps size
matters, but, for humanity, it may just be inversely.

So I built my little house and lived in that marina in
the center of town and sat on the docks and drank beer and
chatted, or barbecued salmon that Fred, the fisherman, had
just caught, and talked until night fell and someone decided
to go for a sail. And I learned to love that ramshackle marina
and those neighbors, so that years later when I had two books
selling well and Candace and I had enough money to buy a
house, the one thing we looked for was a genuine neighborhood where we could feel at home.

We found the smallest of them all.

Deep in the rugged Coastal Mountains of British
Columbia there were two big lakes, and lots of creeks and
falls, and breathtaking scenery. It was only an hour and a half
from Vancouver, had been just woods and farms until ten
years before, but it was near the end of the road and felt as
safe as the end of the world. The yearly snowfall often

reached 30 feet, so someone built a ski-lift and created the longest vertical drop ski run in North America. It was Whistler.

The town was barely a town then: a school, a few stores, two hotels, three restaurants, a chapel, and, for when prayer didn't pay off, a pub. Around the lakes and up the slopes lived a few hundred people, mostly in self-built cabins. They were there because they loved the mountains and the snow and other people.

Most were happy to get by, working the lifts a little, doing some reforestation, tending bar or swinging a hammer, but not too much, so they could concentrate on skiing, or fishing or climbing or sitting in the nearby hot springs until they turned to mush.

No one ever got rich and no one really cared. They could buy a bit of land for ten thousand dollars and, with the help of friends, build themselves a cottage and be set for life except for food, a ski pass, and the occasional piece of wire to hold together the old VW.

It was easy to feel that we instantly belonged.

Benton MacKaye, the father of the Appalachian Trail, felt that for man to lead a wholesome life, in harmony with himself and the world, he would need to have around him a town, working farmland, and lots of wilderness. This should come as no surprise. Since earliest times we have been village dwellers, and it left deep and permanent impressions in our minds. Just as we have an ingrained love for fire, whose heat is so essential for survival, so we seem to yearn deeply for the warmth of a small town.

We seem to long for the shaded streets, small houses, gnarled fruit trees, and vegetable gardens, where doors are never locked and the shop keepers know us, and the town cop knows us, and you stop and chat with everyone because what else is life for? And when the church bell tolls, you go home for lunch, then out to work your garden, and it's a swell place to be a kid, and perfect for a family, and reassuring to grow old and when you have to go, what better place to rest.

If we all love such small towns—and surveys say that seven out of ten of us would live there if we could—why then are they ever more difficult to find? The demand is there, so where is the supply? When all it takes is a few good-natured people—a couple to teach school, a few to run the stores, some to farm the land, some to mend the sick and a bar to tend the healthy—then why isn't there such a town behind every tree? I mean, no one I know dreams of fast food chains and strip malls, yet the world is covered with them; hardly anyone dreams of endless suburbs and freeways, yet we're choking on the stuff. How did it happen that the things no one wants are burying us all, while the simple town we dream of we can seldom find?

What is all this? Really.

6 ~ WHAT SMALL TOWNS
GIVE US

*Polls continue to suggest a real preference among many
Americans for small town life. The desire to retreat from big city
stresses and hazards, the desire to live in a community where one
can be known and make a difference, and a safer environment
for raising children and a desire to be closer to nature all have
contributed to the appeal of rural areas.*
—Kenneth Johnson, Carsey Institute
Report on Rural America

There has been an encouraging rebirth of some North
American small towns in recent years, particularly those
located in areas of dramatic natural beauty—the more scenic
areas of the west coast, the upper Great Lakes region, the pic-
turesque northeast coast including the severe climate of
Down East Maine, the mild climates of the stiff-joints-
friendly coast from Virginia to Florida, and even the foothills
of the Appalachian mountains.

Of the five reasons cited in *The Carsey Report* for seeking out small towns, any one should be sufficient to dislodge us from our cities, but, when combined, they make a compelling case for hitching up the wagon and heading out. I think it worthwhile spending three chapters examining each on its own.

Retreat from Big City Dangers and Stress

I'm not a complete wimp. In the streets of post-war Budapest, fending for yourself was part of surviving. When I was ten, we started a revolution against the Soviet oppression. Armed with bottles filled with gasoline and lit wicks—instantly nicknamed Molotov cocktails—we fought giant Soviet tanks and pushed the Red Army out of Hungary. For eight days we were free. But they returned, with fighter jets and 2,000 new tanks, and bombed and blasted us until the city was half rubble and we ran out of gasoline. And bottles. They were glorious but deadly times.

One day during the fighting I snuck out from the apartment where I lived with my grandparents to get a closer look. I ended up in crossfire outside the headquarters of the secret police. I ran for cover. There was a burnt out truck. I dove under it. Beside me lay two bodies, carbonized except for the whites of their soles. So I'm used to ugliness. But the first time I drove into the smog of LA and saw the eight-lane freeways with a million cars heading in one direction and a million in the other, and we sat in crawling traffic, and although I was only passing through on my way to Mexico instead of spending a lifetime doing this every day, I remember the depression that descended over me and I said to my girlfriend, "This isn't human."

And ever since then, when I visit cities with their numbing noise and traffic, frantic pace, and interchangeable neighborhoods whose people have ennui etched into their faces, etched by the dispiriting repetition of daily commute, job, and exhausted evenings, I often ask myself: Why don't *they* rebel?

The answer perhaps lies in the candid response a dear friend gave one night in New York City. She has a powerful job in publishing and is seemingly fearless, insightful, and incisive. When I mentioned these qualities to her, she said, "Oh. I am all those in my office. But outside of that little world, I feel pretty lost."

Perhaps this is why we remain—discontent in the city, but fearful outside it.

Or it's just as possible that we are so trapped on the relentless treadmill of the consumer life—work—debt—more work—more debt—that we simply cannot find a way to get off. In fact, we may differ only in the details from the hundreds of thousands of workers who, in the early twentieth century, enticed by the promise of sudden fortune in the rubber trade, dove into the jungles of the Amazon. David Grann describes their fate: "Instead of fortune they found that they were indebted to the rubber barons who had provided them with transportation, food and equipment on credit. Wearing a miner's lamp to help him see, a trapper would hack through the jungle, toiling from sunrise to sundown, searching for rubber trees, then upon his return, hungry and feverish, would spend hours hunched over a fire, inhaling toxic smoke as he cooked the latex over a spit until it coagulated. It often took weeks to produce a single rubber ball large enough to sell. And it was rarely enough to discharge his debt. The Brazilian writer Euclides da Cunha noted that the rubber trapper "actually comes to embody a gigantic contradiction; he is a man working to enslave himself."

~

It might be simplistic to suggest that our cities alone, by the fact that they physically threaten us, emotionally bludgeon us, socially neglect us, and financially entrap us, are directly responsible for our spiritual malaise. But then again, who knows? We know for certain that a child's personality is largely shaped by his environment, by how it responds to him, respects him, or ignores him; so it's fairly safe to assume that our stressful, uncaring, impersonal cities generate what Freud called "cultural urges" that may have caused "the whole of mankind to have become neurotic."

That big cities are so stressful and, for lack of a better word, "inhuman" should come as no surprise. Much like cigarettes, quarter-pounders, slums, and heroin, our cities were not created for overall human satisfaction; rather, they grew primarily to render higher profits.

After the final sacking of Rome in 472 by unpaid

Roman troops, the population, which some say had reached 3 million at its height, dwindled to less than 50,000 by the end of that century. We lived without mega cities for millennia, the great migration to them coming in the first half of the nineteenth century with the boom of the Industrial Revolution. Before then, Europe was predominantly or overwhelmingly rural, with 90 percent of Spaniards and 95 percent of Russians living in the country. Until then, manufacturing was local—the cottage industries—and in small workshops close to the water power that propelled machinery. Cities grew and multiplied once the steam engine made it practical to bring together large concentrations of men, women, and children to work in giant factories. With the efficiency of mass manufacture combined with a vast local demand for goods, the isolated cottage industries could no longer compete; they were driven out of existence by the efficiency of numbers just as McDonald's and Home Depot ended the lives of the Mom and Pop restaurant and local hardware store. What an enormous price we paid in both creativity and security with their loss, I will bring up later.

Hence, most cities grew not because the wisest minds set out to build the ideal center for human habitation, where individuals and families could thrive and develop under the safest and best possible conditions, incorporating the maximum amount of natural beauty, parks, squares, and fresh air. Instead, cities were built in haphazard fits and starts, with commerce given priority, and the people squeezed in helterskelter, where they fit, thereafter.

Of course, one may say that commerce is people, or, to broaden the old GM dictum, "What's good for commerce is good for humanity," but I think the financial fiasco of recent times has buried such simple-minded thinking for a while.

Yet, sadly, our cities remain focused on commerce: we have fabulous towers where money is made, impressive buildings where it's kept, glittering shops where it's spent, and clubs and restaurants where it is flashed, and we have endless acres for cars to speed or rest, but where is the space for the physical, social, and—I don't mean to sound maudlin—the spiritual needs of the people? Where is the inviting space for mothers to stroll with their infants? Where are the ample clean places to watch toddlers play? Where is there space for older kids to spend their rambunctious energy? Where are the schools within a comfortable but stimulating walk or bike ride from home? Where are the informal public spaces for adolescents to meet (and please don't equate private malls or fast food joints to a park or public square)? Where can one, during the turbulent years of adolescence, go to find the comforting solitude of nature? And where can young lovers find romantic places of natural beauty, where they can experience that magical sensation that there is no one in the world but them? Where can neighbors stroll and meet each other casually, spontaneously, and spend time talking, gossiping, exchanging ideas, being friends? And where can old people spend their precious time being constructive, passing on wisdom, being part of society? To almost every question, our cities answer, "Nowhere."

And if all the above sound like "extras" to our modern minds, then that's doubly sad, for they are simple things that small towns still provide. And they were—and in a few socially aware cities still are—among the most thought out and revered parts of life.

And while there are some benefits to the anonymity of city life, that same anonymity causes us to be emotional hermits full of the anxiety and suspicion that's inherent to being alone. For, in most cases, we seldom know our neighbors, often our co-workers are but casual acquaintances, and even our friendships tend to be non-spontaneous, scheduled events. When we need the help of another human being, be that someone to watch the kids, or fix the door, or just to help us unburden our soul, we pay. When we need a laugh we rent a movie, when we need security we pay a guard, when we need a friend we pay a shrink. So little by little we get ingrained to the fact that if we want anything from anyone it's going to cost us cash. When we are thus trained to see the world in monetary terms, it's understandable that we become anxious, defensive, and always vigilant to make sure we get the correct change from Life.

So no city dweller should feel bad about being stressed; he should in fact feel bad if he wasn't. For cities, just like advertising, prey on our anxieties; we feel aimless, so we buy something; we feel isolated at home, so we go eat in a restaurant; we want to be among friends, so we go out among strangers and for a moment feel a flickering but fake sense that we belong. Well, we don't. Which brings us to the second reason people love small towns.

To Live Where You are Known

Perhaps I'm overly sensitive, but I suffer from a hollow feeling, somewhat akin to being lost, when I'm living in the enormous anonymity of New York, Paris, or Rome, where no one knows you, whether in your apartment building, local stores, or even your local bar.

And, in sharp contrast, how reassuring it feels to walk through our medieval town, where people greet you, where both butchers know you, and Giovanna the baker knows you, and Marzia the fishwife knows exactly what you need before you even thought it, and everyone in the bank knows you and the advice they give you is usually sensible and from the heart, and even those in the tiny supermarket know you and the plumber and carpenter and doctor all know you, and even the Chief of Police, the *vigili* knows you, although that doesn't stop the heartless bastard from giving you a ticket when you're double-parked.

These daily encounters rarely carry earth-shaking revelations, or ground-breaking discussions on Nietzsche, and only seldom even juicy gossip. Sometimes they're occasions for an espresso or glass of wine, but most often they're just a greeting or a handshake or a smile, or a few words, a few questions, or a jibe, but that seems to suffice. It seems enough to make you remember you're part of the world around you, that you are perhaps a tiny but vital part of your hometown.

One of the most moving Tuscan traditions, the outpouring of the true affection your townspeople feel for you, unfortunately you will not witness.

There are six active churches in our hilltop town, scattered inside the walls, down winding, stone-paved streets, or at the bottom of arch-covered stairways, but it is the church of La Madonna, set among open greenery on the ramparts of the town, where the town turns out to pay you its last respects. It's a good-sized church from the sixteenth century, with a calm Renaissance façade of pale marble, and the townspeople fill it and most often overflow onto the road and *piazzetta* before it—never fewer than two hundred, and, if you were well-loved, maybe five. At no funeral have I seen fake solemnity, just the emotion however deep they felt for you while alive, and kids walk in and out during the mass, while some people softly chatter and others distractedly fiddle with their watches.

At the end the priest, swinging burning incense, heads out of the church, followed by your friends carrying your coffin into the afternoon air. On foot, everyone follows the open hearse south on the road closed for the occasion, under the big ilex trees along the western ramparts. They walk in a long, curving line four or five abreast, while the bell tolls in the misty light, walk a good half mile below the *fortezza*, past the bluff, and turn below the *carabinieri* for your last quarter mile.

The cemetery is in the hillside, with graves on terraces or in the stone wall under the cypresses. Your friends lower you into the ground, then, while the townspeople stand on the terraces all around, with worn shovels, throw the dirt over you.

Afterward they drift to a cafe or bar, and they sip and reminisce about what a grand fellow you were, or, if not quite grand, the *vigili* say, at least no worse than Mussolini.

Where You Make a Difference

There is little in city life that tells us we are unique, indispensable individuals who contribute something essential to the world.

As for suburbia, no one has penned our plight there better than Lewis Mumford. Perhaps our most noted historian of technology and science, he was an authority on urban life, and architecture critic for *The New Yorker* for 30 years. He lamented eloquently but with brutal forthrightness about suburbia: "We have created a featureless landscape of featureless people. A green ghetto half natural, half plastic, cut off from human contact, where the wife has for her chief daily companions the radio, the soap opera, the refrigerator, the blender, the vacuum cleaner, the washing machine, the car." It is a place where family members gather after work and "together or by turns immobilize themselves before a television screen, where all that has been left out of the actual world, all their unlived life, flickers before their eyes."

And while most suburbs do provide physical security, they do precious little to satisfy social needs, and next to nothing to encourage us to be anything but strangers who happen to park their cars on the same street every night.

In short, our urban and suburban existence only very rarely reminds us that we, in some way, "make a difference." This is no small thing. I'll never forget Paolucci's face when he said that it was "good to be needed," and that was coming from someone who gets daily appreciation from his family and friends for providing tangible goods he either grew or raised or made himself: a slab of *prosciutto* from the attic, or a basket of fruit and vegetables from the *orto*, or a jug of wine from the cellar. Just imagine how much most of us, who, at best, bring home store-bought goods or a check, must miss "being needed."

Small towns, on the other hand, literally bloom with opportunities to make us feel constructive, unique, and making some difference almost daily. The hamlet of Camigliano might serve as a classic example of the ideal microcosm that provided what Mumford called "social efficiency and overall human satisfaction." Camigliano lies nine miles southwest of Montalcino. At the entrance of town is the cemetery; small, walled, and meticulously kept, with flowers on every grave, even Giuliano Sorbi's, who's been a permanent here for over forty years. One grave, simply inscribed "La Mamma Martina," is planted like a miniature garden, with rocks, tiny cypresses, and a tiny olive.

The hamlet has a castle, a church, and only a couple

dozen houses, yet it has three *piazze* filled with sunlight, fresh air, and voices. From the main *piazza*, a long stone ramp leads down to the town's dome-covered well.

Until the late sixties, when government-sponsored industrialization of cities began to coax people from the countryside, Camigliano was abuzz with seventy noisy Tuscans. There was Don Otello, the diminutive but feisty grappa-making priest; two schoolteachers in the schoolhouse on the bluff, where some kids went in the morning and others after lunch to best utilize the space; and Beppetto the cabinetmaker in his workshop at *piazza*'s end, next to Donato Sorbi, blacksmith, Quinto Gorelli, shoemaker, and Aldo Sorbi, the town's fix-everything mechanic.

Beppetto could fabricate doors and windows, or pews for the church, or a barrel for the cellar, a walnut table or a chestnut trunk for your wedding, and even a fine poplar box for that big day at the end.

Donato shoed mules and horses, made wrought iron railings, galvanized tin buckets and big copper cauldrons, and made pitchforks, hay rakes, spades, and even knives. Then he washed up for dinner, downed a good meal, and, in a cellar near the well, opened up the door of his *osteria*, where the town and countryside gathered to sip wine and play cards or the accordion.

Aldo fixed bicycles, clocks, pumps, and thrashers, while his cousin Donato not only resoled old shoes but also cobbled new ones, cutting the thick soles and pounding the uppers to shape, then sewing them together with bold stitches by hand. A pair of his shoes would last you all your life.

Near the well was a restaurant with three tables and a corner of shelves loaded with groceries. Here, Olga cooked up mouth-watering meals and her son in law Mireno, like some well-fed Basil Fawlty, ran the bar. Behind the church in a grassy clearing, where in the hamlet's great brick oven everyone baked their bread, were two small shops side by side, one selling bolts of cloth, the other buttons, laces, wool, needles, and thread. Finished clothes you had to buy in Montalcino on Fridays, when the market opened up in the streets of town. Or you waited for Menconi.

Menconi came down from Siena once a month. He came on his *motorino* Beta 48, the kind of motorbike you had to peddle up a slope and push up every hill, and stopped for a day in each hamlet and town. You could see Menconi coming from miles away. He wound among the green hills in a great heap of colors like an elephant dressed for carnival, because his *motorino* had been rigged with clothes racks all around, leaving just an opening for Menconi's goggled eyes. And from these racks fluttered shirts, pants, skirts, aprons, and dresses, and long scarves, hats, and suits, and every other kind of clothing you could ever think to wear.

With his clothes he brought gossip. That night he would sleep on some clean hay in a barn—cows and goats were precious then, their stalls cleaned twice a day—while the hamlet stayed awake mulling over the fresh gossip Menconi had brought.

And the next day the men discussed it in the fields or

woods, the women in the cellars or at the big *forno*, where each household took its weekly turn bringing bundles of dry broom or the twigs from the forest. They would fire up the big domed brick oven until the bricks in its ceiling turned white, then in would go great heaps of leavened dough and trays of pastry, and out would come golden Tuscan loaves with a crust like stone that would keep the inside of the bread fresh all through the week. In summer, the women stood beside the church to catch the breeze that funneled there; in winter, they huddled near the heated bricks and watched the snowflakes fall.

And every few days they would meet up at the *lavatoio*, the local place to do laundry. Under a roof shored by stone columns was running water, stone sinks, and sloped stones where you pounded your clothes with a stick or your fist depending on how much your husband had busted your balls last night. Then you'd hang your blinding shirts and sheets to billow like flags of victory in the breeze.

Between the daily chores were life's great events. The whole town turned out for baptisms, first communions, confirmations, graduations, weddings, and the rest, each event followed by a massive all-day feast.

And if all that didn't provide enough of a sense of inclusion with friends and acquaintances who appreciated you, around whom you felt helpful and at ease, then there were always those great masculine gatherings from October to February: The Boar Hunts.

Each hunt involves a *squadra*, or team, of fifty men and

many dogs.

To avoid deadly accidents, each *squadra* had a hunting ground with clear, definite borders and no adjoining ground is hunted the same day. This is vital because hunters here don't wear orange gear for safety—much too practical—they wear *dark camouflage* to blend into the landscape. Until they move. At which point, in the dark scrub, they look just like a boar.

Then it's bang, bang; dearly beloved; RIP; Amen.

The boar hunt begins at dawn, with fifty cold and sleepy men knocking back grappa to jump-start the heart. They set up in a vast circle around where the boars are known to be, and the dog handlers let loose the dogs and heard them toward the *posti*, the men with the guns.

Each *posto* stands where he knows every bush, each rock, and hence the path the boar is likely to take running for its life. They stand there like statues, freezing their asses off, not allowed to move even to scratch their privates, because the boar might notice them and go the other way and then they will have stood there all morning for nothing.

In a good year, the *squadra* brings home three boar per hunter. After discarding the head, bones and hide, each hunter can take home a hundred pounds of meat. Much of it is eaten fresh but some is made into *prosciutto* or mixed with pork—to compensate for boar meat's hardness—into small sausages, then hung in the attic to dry.

Not long ago the hunt was for survival. Considering

that Tuscans of old ate meat but once a week, with polenta or pasta and vegetables as their staples, wild boar, hare, pheasants, and quail made up a good portion of the Tuscan way of life.

~

In Tuscan towns, your wealth counts for little—it can actually raise disdain. It's how much you add to the town that counts. So Giovanna the baker, and Carlo the butcher, and Di Stefano the Pharmacist or Adriano the stone mason, are each as indispensable as the other; the whole town would turn out to walk their last mile with them.

I have singled out no women of the town. There seems no need; they *are* the town, as respected, revered, and more needed than God. They not only feed their families daily meals that visitors from around the world recall for life, but they are mothers and grandmothers and the family bankers, and nurses and psychologists and policeman of their realm. And they know it.

~

So if we were to look down from a rooftop of Camigliano, into its *piazza*s, its gardens, its small shops, *forno*, and the *lavatoio*, and see Donato with his door open cobbling a new shoe, or Don Otello in his back garden running his little still, we would see each of its citizens in a special space, in a unique role, each contributing to the whole. It would be easy to conclude that with all this *personal* exchange of services, goods, and some daily kindness, everyone's role in the hamlet's life is vital. And it is this "counting," this being an integral part of daily life, that allows you to sleep fulfilled every night, and to awaken happy every morning.

And this counting, this being needed, binds together neighborhoods and quarters, hamlets and towns, making them places to cherish, to belong to. Making them home.

7 ~ A SAFE ENVIRONMENT
FOR RAISING CHILDREN

We live seven twisting miles from Montalcino, so Buster would often ask to stay in town after school to play. When I had errands, I'd drop by at the last bell to tell him where we'd meet and when. I saw right off that the parents whose kids lived within the town walls seldom came to pick up their *tesoro*. Kids as young as seven would charge alone out of the schoolyard and up to the park or into the *campino*, a little field next door, or wander up the main street of town—closed to traffic—to play ball in the *piazza* and drive all the tourists mad.

When it rained, the kids hung out under the arches, or they would sit in one of the little shops owned by their parents or parents of friends, doing homework, helping out, or running the odd errand for a newspaper or a *panino* from the bar.

After a while I learned that if you wanted to find your kid, you just walked down the street and asked around. You'd ask the shopkeepers, or the *vigili,* or the *spazzino* who swept the stone streets with his long and curvy broom, or the old gents in the *piazza* playing cards at tables outside the bar, or the baker, or Petto in Piazza Padella who sold pizza by the slice and sooner or later would be visited by every kid in town. Somebody would have seen your kid and know exactly where to find him.

But a town's responsibility for a child's security is much more complex than just keeping track or making sure he won't get run over by a car. Just as your neighbors in the countryside make you feel secure, so, to an even greater extent, does a Tuscan town.

First there is your extended home. Since many parents work in town, their shops and offices become second homes to children. The homes and workplaces of other relatives and friends are even better, for they provide all the gooey sweets your mother forbids at home.

And informal hanging out in workplaces allows children to learn, and not only about making change or wrapping packages. They get to witness interactions between owners, workers, and clients, and by watching how people treat each other, help each other, and solve problems together, they learn to listen, to be helpful, to be kind. They learn that a business exchange is not just about money, but that it's a social event between different people. And the more kids learn how to "handle" people, the more they learn to see another's point of view, the more confident and secure they will feel in life.

And most children thrive in adult situations where they have a sense of being useful or needed. Buster was a lover of chores from early life; he helped the stonemasons clean old tiles, or the baker load bread, or he swept a local bar, or got underfoot in the kitchens of the restaurant serving water, or baskets of bread, or translating the menu for *stranieri*. And he'd invariably end his "work" with a self-satisfied smile.

~

This participating in real life not only increases a child's respect for himself and others, but also provides a more complex view of people whom they otherwise might have known only on the surface. Take teachers as an example. In most school situations, a teacher represents authority and kids obey commands. It is a well-defined, functional, but limited relationship. Kids form a narrow view of teachers, often based on the strictness of their manner or the marks they give. But in small towns, kids encounter teachers in *piazze*, streets, and stores, and can see them in the roles of "normal" people—less forbidding, more frail, more human. And these short encounters allow for a new view of each other not limited by roles, or fear, or restriction of time. Not only does this give kids a broader perspective of people in general, but it also allows them to form stronger bonds. Getting to know their teacher as a friend suddenly broadens the space where they feel "safe."

~

Once in a while, a teacher can affect a town for generations. Maestro Tonino was one of them. Tall, gaunt, and elegant—Fellini would have loved him for a role—he was consistently affable and intensely witty. He had, at one time or other, taught nearly everyone in town. He had been teaching for thirty years when we moved to Montalcino, but as admired as he was in school, he was an even more monumental symbol outside it. In his colorful cravat and with his raincoat over his shoulder, he would sit at a table of the Fiaschetteria, the old Liberty-style cafe in the main *piazza*, reading, writing, or just talking with every adult or child that happened to stop by. From a distance, Maestro Tonino seemed to be holding court. He'd pass out bits of encouragement or wisdom or sharp, snappy abuse, depending on what he judged would work best at the moment, his long hands slicing the air for emphasis and his quick laughter bouncing off the walls around the square. He was the last of the Romantics, with an aesthete's view of life and art, food and wine; an excellent cook and a great dinner companion who could electrify a table or unify the town.

He was Buster's teacher for years—the same two teachers followed a class from grade one on through five—and he was as effective as he was loved. He was ruthless with his students—no favors and no nonsense. But his every thoughtful word would count and most would be remembered. The whole town seemed to darken when he died. The streets before the church filled for his funeral. Classes he had taught brought wreaths and stood shoulder to shoulder just like they had in the hallway thirty years before. And when the old priest rose to remember Tonino, speaking of when they were young in the streets kicking a ball against the wall, he had to stop often and for a while, to catch his voice and wipe his eyes, and the church and the streets filled with sniffles and sighs.

And a river of people followed his coffin under the trees along the ramparts of the town.

And the students of his last class—twelve years ago, now—the roughest and most ornery he said of all his life, still get together for a big feast every year to eat and drink and talk about Tonino, that fastidious, exacting wit with whom an era died, but who will live forever in their memories and their hearts.

~

Although our town is perched atop a steep hill, among its winding rows of houses there is a remarkable amount of open public space. Inside the *fortezza* is a big shaded garden, outside is a terraced playground underneath great pines; each church has a *piazzetta* before it, and the Madonna has a stretch of gardens on either side. There is the *giardino* at the lower end of town, and our two big *piazze*, Padella and Popolo, and there is open space around the old wash places and below the southern walls that ring the town, and a wide walkway that is filled on sunny days, the benches there offering sunsets to die for.

Most of the town streets are closed to traffic—and not

just the main street, where bars and restaurants expanded to outdoors, but more permanently the ones too steep or too narrow—some only long stairways. So, if you're a kid, the whole town is your playground. The darkened archways, the dead-end secret places are yours to discover, to play chase in, to hide in. And when you grow older and love invades your life, there are quiet public places—every nook and cranny has a stone wall or a bench—where you can peacefully experience the first physical bliss of tumultuous passions.

I am always amazed by the teenagers of our town; they seem to have perfected a life of hanging out. They wander about in pairs or in flowing and ebbing flocks, from one space to the next—always on foot—only to settle in and continue their laughter and endless conversations. And it's not uncommon to hear groups of them singing softly in the night.

Just how strong and lasting the bonds are between them seems remarkable to me. Even though Buster has been away at school for the last six years, his friendships here have grown only stronger. They are instant on his return and constant through his stay. Whether it's with his best friend Giulia, the pharmacists daughter, or Matteo, who was his best pal in grade school, or just the rest of the "gang" that hung around, their summer nights are spent walking the town together, or coming down to our house on hot days for swims or noisy cook outs in the garden, where they get pleasantly and entertainingly drunk. From weekends at the seashore to long country walks, for him these friendships are a sustaining part of life. And although he's happy enough alone at most times, he really blooms when the whole gang's around.

~

It is this infinite number of small but continuous ties that makes small towns in Tuscany a heaven for children.

As far as I can tell, here lies true security. When help or encouragement or consolation or laughter is always so nearby, when you're always sought out and wanted for work or play, isn't it then just child's play to navigate through life?

No visitor to Tuscany fails to remark on how easygoing and happy Tuscans are. Theirs is a genuine warmth, the exuberance of children that has somehow stayed with them, that has somehow survived.

A Childhood for our Children

In modern urban life, kids are too often either a precious accessory to flaunt or radioactive waste with no safe place to dump. In small-town Tuscany, even though loved to death, they're allowed to fit into society where they fall.

A child brought up active in daily life will often shock you with patience, originality, and wit, and can often be more entertaining than the adults they drag along. If, on the other hand, they're raised as a cutesy pet or, much worse, in exile surrounded by lifeless gadgets, they are likely to turn out antisocial and self-obsessed, with no more interest in social intercourse than a turtle has in tango.

~

We had the Paoluccis over for *pranzo* one recent Sunday. Of course it was a meal that took days of preparation. Our friend Nunzi made pasta by hand for two kinds of lasagna, one with zucchini and the other with a sauce of mixed pork and veal; and we made three kinds of spreads to put on the *crostini*: chopped *porcini* stir-fried with olive oil, garlic, and parsley; ground walnuts mixed with butter and anchovy; and grilled sausage crumbled and blended with Certosa cheese. The *scottiglia* of pork and chicken stewed for hours, and only the ribs and *radicchio* remained to be grilled.

The Paoluccis didn't come so much as they invaded. There were three generations: mom and dad, their two daughters with husbands, and three children from ages three to ten.

We all sat together and ate with good china and wine glasses and everyone talked about the same amount until, biting into the lasagna, Martina, the six-year old, called out, "Candace, this is the best pasta I ever ate in my life." Then Niccolo, ten years old, sipped his half glass of wine, turned seriously to Candace, and said, *"Buono anche questo. Complimenti."*

~

That Friday night we went to the thirty-seventh birthday party of a friend. Twelve of us were thirty-seven and up, but the thirteenth, Gea, had recently turned nine. Neither we nor Gea seemed to give a damn. It was a buffet dinner, so groups formed and dissolved and reformed again, and Gea dissolved and reformed with them. She chatted and asked and laughed, and the only reason she stood out was because she stood a little lower. It was a crowd of architects, artists, doctors, photographers, editors, engineers, and even a professional pilot of hot-air balloons—in other words, people pretty full of themselves—yet no one talked down to her or babied her or treated her like anything but an intelligent and entertaining—albeit short—person, and only once in the four hours, when an adult joke was begun, was she told to go out and find the cat.

~

Last year, between Christmas and New Years, we had six house guests for a week. A composer and his doctor wife, whose children had grown, came alone, and Giovanna came with three teenagers, so we ranged from fourteen up to sixty-three. The lunches and dinners were all long affairs, and I honestly can't say anyone dominated the conversation, although Giovanna and I have been known to talk each other to death. A couple of evenings all of us played *panforte*, an ancient Tuscan game where you take a wrapped, hard fruitcake and try to slide it close to the table's distant edge.

I have never seen kids having so much fun. They screamed and shrieked, laughingly cheated and competed, and played with profound joy for hours.

Admittedly these are Tuscan kids who, as I said, had a sociable upbringing. They are close to the variety that so impressed anthropologist Jared Diamond during the time he spent in New Guinea. In his Pulitzer Prize-winning book *Guns, Germs, and Steel,* he writes, "My perspective comes from 33 years of working with New Guineans in their own intact societies. From the very beginning they impressed me as being on the average more intelligent, more alert, more expressive, and more interested in things and people around them than the average European or American is . . .

"Modern European and American children spend much of their time being passively entertained by television, radio and movies. In the average American household the TV set is on for seven hours per day. In contrast, traditional New Guinea children have virtually no such opportunities for passive entertainment and instead spend almost all of their waking hours actively doing something, such as talking or playing with other children or adults. Almost all studies of child development emphasize the role of childhood stimulation and activity in promoting mental development, and stress the irreversible mental stunting associated with reduced childhood stimulation. This effect surely contributes a non-genetic component to the superior average mental function displayed by New Guineans.

"That is, in mental ability New Guineans are probably genetically superior to Westerners, and they surely are superior in escaping the devastating developmental disadvantages under which most children in industrialized societies grow up."

∼

And not only is constant interaction a vital part of development, but so is being left free to invent "spontaneous play." Penny Wilson, a consultant on play projects on both sides of the Atlantic, made this disturbing observation:

"Play is an instinctive and essential part of childhood, which is becoming more and more under pressure, with evidence that a lack of spontaneous play leaves a long-term social legacy. Play allows children to work out their emotions. When you're playing you're finding out about who you are...The world of play is being encroached. There are ambitious middle-class parents who over-schedule their children's lives—so there is no time left for children to play their own imaginative games.

"And with many of the toys we buy, the toys do the playing, not the child. Play should not be based on ownership. The consumerist approach has taken away the initiative from children.

"I'm really frightened about that generation of children who are growing up without having played. I did a play session in Manhattan with a class of eight-year-olds and the children went completely crazy, bashing things up, they didn't know what to do with themselves."

∼

The Tuscan-style inclusion of children in real life is not just for them, it's for us. Not only can they be disarmingly charming, but they also refresh with their candidness and views. And *all* of us gain from socially well-rounded children, because the more knowledgeable they are about a variety of people, the more interesting, more confident, and more morally aware they will become. And all this contact and interaction with family, friends, and neighbors may just possibly kindle their interest in humans. Real humans, not the imitation ones on TV with fake, simplistic responses to fake situations, but unscripted, spontaneous ones. And among this fragile, complex, sad, or joyous lot, they might just find some real heroes—vulnerable, ever changing, puzzling, messy ones, whom you can hate like hell one minute and love like hell the next, who might just give them some idea of what they might like, and might not like, to grow up to be.

And the more varied the people they mingle with, in age, character, health, wealth, background, views, and needs, the richer will be their learning, the deeper their understanding, and the more unquenchable their thirst for learning more. Because the most profound and lasting lessons in life they will learn not from videos or books or even the internet, but from direct contact with this admittedly chaotic, but endlessly entertaining, humanity.

It takes people to teach people to be people.

8 ~ CLOSE TO NATURE

One touch of nature makes the whole world kin.
　　　　　—William Shakespeare, *Troilus and Cressida*

Some winters ago, when I was behind on two books—a memoir and a book of photographs—I hired an assistant to organize and edit the first, and help design the latter. She was New York City-born and raised, in her late twenties, with an Ivy League masters degree, serious, dedicated, if somewhat diffident. She loved words, had an amazing eye for color and design, and had laser-like concentration. She came to Tuscany for a month so that, removed from all distraction, we could slave away undisturbed. When I picked her up at the Rome airport, with her flat hair and stiff gait, she looked like a delegate to the convention of Librarians of the Sacred Heart.

　　　Both editing a manuscript and choosing and cropping photographs are mentally and emotionally exhausting. Even though we took long, relaxed lunches by the fire in our kitchen, by mid afternoon her eyes would grow squinty, her pale skin gaunt, and her mouth tight from tension and fatigue. With her big cheek bones and translucent skin, she seemed a death mask. By the third afternoon, I thought I'd made a mistake choosing such a high-strung city girl—her boyfriend had broken up with her the month before and that weighed on her, too—and, almost out of sheer frustration, I told her to go out for a walk in the country. Reluctantly, she obeyed.

It was a clear, crisp, slightly frosty day. She went with her shoulders hunched, through the vineyards, past the church, toward the cypresses of the old cemetery. She stayed away an hour, returning as the sun set. She had changed. Her blue eyes were blazing, her cheeks ruddy, and her mouth relaxed into a smile. "It worked," she said.

From that day on, she took a walk each afternoon, through the fields or woods, the olive grove or the canyon, and by the second week that blazing, healthy look became permanent day and night. Even though her dedication to work never wavered—I called her "The *Ubermeister* of the Pleasure *Polizei*"—an irrepressible humor bubbled out of her; at times I laughed so hard I had cramps behind my ears. By the time she left, she was unrecognizable: open, sloppy, and warm, and even her face had changed; she looked almost wild. The *Ubermeister* had bloomed.

A few days later, I was on the phone to a friend in New York and asked how she seemed on her return. The answer was, "She beamed." When she next saw the boyfriend, he fell back in love at first sight.

Living amidst nature in Tuscany does that to you, turns you inside out, brings out an inner richness you never knew you had—consuming half your body weight in wine doesn't hurt either, but then that, too, is part of nature in Tuscany.

~

There is something about the benevolent aspect of the Tuscan countryside that on the one hand, calms, and on the other, turns wild. It may be the mix of hamlets, vineyards, fields, and gnarled woods, a blend of civilization and wilderness entangled.

And it affects you no matter how long you've lived here, as if every day you saw the world with brand new eyes. I honestly cannot remember a time when, no matter how angry or frustrated I had been in the house with work, bureaucracy, the weather, or all of life, an hour's work outside or just a walk didn't turn my mood right around.

And no matter how bad a fight I have with Candace, by the time I reach the bluff where the waterfall tumbles I cannot imagine having a better wife. And I say to myself, "This is paradise."

Extolling the restorative power of nature, Emerson wrote, "In the woods is perpetual youth...A decorum and sanctity reign, a perennial festival is dressed, and a guest sees not how he should tire of them in a thousand years. In the woods we return to reason and to faith."

These revivals through nature should come as no surprise: we lived close to her for millennia; she left an indelible imprint on our memory. Not only has she nurtured and protected us, but, from Emerson's point of view, she has left us in a state of wonder. Yet as spiritually satisfying as glimpses of nature are, "each moment of the year has its own beauty, and in the same field, it beholds every hour, a picture which was never seen before, and which shall never be seen again," Emerson's view of nature is but that of an urban spectator coming across something aesthetically pleasing. For Tuscans, there is a more complex reward.

Ofelio, our neighbor down the hill, turned seventy-four this year. When you sit with him inside, sipping a glass of wine, he complains about the wear and tear the years have left behind, how this aches and that hurts, how he's no longer young. But let him out into the fields and woods, where he still spends most his life, and he will move with a speed and agility of someone half his age, someone used to moving with the freedom of the wild.

And as I struggle to keep up with him along a rising path, I too become more limber, my steps more varied, joints more supple: I come alive.

Striding behind him I still see bits of beauty—the startling colors of leaves, a twisted ilex trunk, a shaft of sunlight through the trees, a rock sculpted with moss, a cascade of tumbling water turning into spray—but I *feel* so much more:

the joy of loping movement, the pride of survival, the titillating fear of the unknown up ahead.

And in Tuscany that beautiful nature, distant and misty or close and musky underfoot, is not just something to behold; it feeds you, keeps you alive.

~

Far up canyon one of our neighbors thinned the woods. It has been done this way for centuries, a few hectares a year, primarily for firewood but also to renew the forest, to cut old growth and deadwood, and to give new shoots a chance at life. At every few paces a mature tree is left, so the forest is still a forest but with lots more light.

The woodcutters carted off the trunks in four-foot lengths, but some slid into the gorge, into the torrent far below. Our forests are hardwood, thus heavy as hell—a four-foot trunk ten inches in diameter can outweigh a bag of cement.

This winter I work in the gorge each morning. A narrow path is notched, forming a ledge, slanting down into the bottom of the gorge. I go down, shoulder a slab of wood, and start back. The path is rocky, steep, slippery, wet; there is a thrill in having to navigate each step. At the shallow point I ford the stream, drop the load in a wheelbarrow, then go back again. Once I have three good trunks, I grab the handles hard and take a running start so I can make it up the rise. Two hundred yards through the woods; all uphill. My leg muscles burn, my heart thrashes, and my mind yells, "Don't be a fool, old man!" But if I stop uphill I'll never start again. My legs wobble and I see stars and I cut a deal with God that if he lets me live this time I'll never do something so stupid again.

At the top I gasp for air but feel exalted, victorious. And, for the moment at least, I proved Joseph Conrad wrong, because I recovered "that feeling" he thought "would never come back any more . . . the triumphant conviction of strength, the heat of life in a handful of dust, the glow in the heart that with every year grows dim, grows cold, grows small and expires—expires, too soon—before life itself."

Not yet, damn it. Not today. Not yet.

Then I pick up the wheelbarrow and turn downhill again. If God mentions the deal, I'll just plead amnesia.

~

And that night in the fireplace in the kitchen, where the fire burns from October through March, the log I hauled out of the canyon sizzles, then turns to flames and coals and roasts the chicken slowly, and after that we make *bruschetta* rubbed with garlic, soak it with fresh-pressed olive oil, and wash it down with wine, and all the while that log heats the house, and pleases the eye, and keep us safe and warm. That piece of wood I nearly killed myself hauling through the forest, over the stream, through the winter light that found its way below. It all feels like life. That nature. The woods. These moments of "perpetual youth."

Candace says that it's the fragrance of the loam that draws her into the forest every day. Whether clearing a path, gathering kindling, or checking one of her favorite spots for chanterelles, she says that smell connects her to the soil, the forest, the land, the world. From most walks she returns with something—mushrooms through the fall, *corbezzolo* berries for jam in December, wild asparagus along the woods' edge in the spring, or wild garlic with pink flowers from the first buds on the vines. But she loves the woods for the changing seasons that let her feel the cycles of life—the birth and death of all things around her. And this from someone as unsentimental as they come, in fact feisty and mean—the only human I know of the feminine persuasion who, in a flare of rage, can drive a hoe through a steel wheelbarrow, then laughingly call it "art."

Roughing it in nature seems frightening—and it should—yet it's amazing how quickly we can de-civilize. I am spoiled and fussy; I like soft sheets, down pillows, hot showers, and sit-down meals with tablecloths, wine glasses, and a cozy fire. Yet the ways of Tuscany—the nature, the land, and, most importantly, living simply, became part of me, gave me a calm I carried with me to the far side of the world.

When our house was almost restored, and when, after a year of twelve-hour days struggling as carpenter, contractor, architect, engineer, mason's helper, ditch digger and all round go-fer, I could not look another stone or brick in the eye, the masons left us for two months: July to rebuild a kitchen for an aunt, and August for their unvaried yearly holiday.

With our money almost gone, we decided to save each penny and spend the summer on a desert island—the three of us, alone.

Twenty miles off Canada's west coast lie the Gulf Islands. They're protected from the rage of the Pacific by a 200-mile hulk called Vancouver Island that creates, to the east of it, a tranquil inland sea.

The islands are woods and rock. Some low land was farmed in the last century, but water is scarce, so the farming all died out, and now the islands are inhabited by recluses, artists, and those who love rocks more than they do people. The ferry ride takes two hours from the mainland, and by the time you arrive in the quiet desolation, with only the sound of eagles' cries above, you'll have forgotten that there are other places on the planet.

Around a body of water called Plumper Sound, three large islands block out the world; only through Winter Pass can you see the glacier of Mount Baker glow pink in the late-day light.

A half-mile from the nearest island, high at its north end and low in the south, with a cluster of ancient firs pointing at the sky, rises Fane Island. It's a thousand feet long and two hundred feet wide, two islands really, with a crescent sandy spit between them guarding a harbor. The southern point is barren rock, with tufts of dry grasses and piles of driftwood that the southeast gales piled up during the winter storms. There is a battered oak near the tip, where eagles perch and watch the sea for fish. The middle of the island is all Garry oak, low, gnarled, twisted, sculpted by the wind, with a thick canopy under which sea otters live, alongside flocks of birds and mink. In the middle of the island towers a thousand-year-old fir, around it some younger ones, and big, shiny-barked arbutus trees in a meadow. Near the harbor is a one-room cottage. It has a wood burning stove, an old wooden table, a couch, and a sleeping loft above.

There is no power on the island or fresh water or a dock, only the pebbly beach or the sandstone rocks for landing. But the tide falls and rises ten feet in six hours, so you have to be sure the skiff won't get washed away or end up high and dry in the morning.

Setting foot on the island, I had the unnerving sensation of living a new life. It seemed frightening. There were no paths. Except for the tiny cottage, the place was wild. All the order and ease I had known seemed far behind. I embraced the cottage: swept it, cleaned it, evicted ants, destroyed cobwebs, scraped away lichen and moss that were slowly reclaiming the land—*anything* just to get a sense that I controlled the place. That evening, we lit the propane stove to boil pasta in a pot forgetting I had just hauled the precious fresh water a mile in a jug. And I tore open the bag of charcoal to grill steak on the Hibachi, with potatoes neatly wrapped in tinfoil, and we set the table with tablecloth and wine glasses, china and silverware, and lit candles on the table and tried to have a dinner like I had all my life. Darkness and silence fell, except for the sea breaking, and it was so romantic with the candles' glow, until the candles gutted and I went to turn on the lights. There were no lights. But outside the window glowed a thunderstorm of stars.

~

It was frightening but exhilarating to be left to our own devices. If anything went wrong—this was before cell phones—fire, storm, or injury, righting it was up to us: our rational thinking, skills, and inventions.

The first nights on the island I didn't sleep so well. I felt anxious and frail; the power of nature felt immense. But each day more confidence seemed to seep into our bones. Without paths we had to bushwhack to the south tip, or scramble over the rocks, at times fording the sea. And all day we did chores: dug a hole for the outhouse, rigged the solar shower and gathered firewood from the beach for the stove because the nights are cold so far north.

The third night we had dinner on the beach. We cooked inside and brought everything down—pots, pans, dishes, cutlery, glasses—to eat by the water with the glow of lantern light.

The next day we were out of meat, so Candace and Buster went fishing. They caught ling cod and rock cod. We thought it would be fun to cook on the beach on the fire, so we fried the fish in a pan and boiled the corn along with some sliced beets. It was a hassle to wash the pots, but the sea was smooth and you didn't need a lantern in the moonlight.

The next night we cooked on the fire without pots. The fish we roasted on a cedar skewer, the corn we threw unshucked onto the coals, and the beets, unskinned, on the hot rocks beside it. The fish guts had drawn in crab, and I flipped them on their backs and killed them with a sharp stone, then tore off the legs and claws, rinsed them in the sea, and threw them onto the coals beside the corn. The corn roasted to perfection, the beets were soft in their skins, the crabmeat was succulent, and the fish tasted smoked and fell off the bones. Sitting on rocks, we ate with our fingers, using driftwood for plates.

We had done it. Forgone civilization. Returned to the Stone Age. Except for the wine.

Between the rough terrain of the island and the quick movement of the skiff, we were always balancing, shifting, walking, rowing, moving. By night we were exhausted. I had never slept so deeply in my life.

By the summer's end, our movements became supple, and in all that time no one slipped or fell, and we moved fast and sure-footedly, even while hauling loads. We rowed the skiff and made friends with a seal pup, and even the sea otters didn't hide when we neared. Only the mink loped away shyly. And all of us recall that summer with the fondest memories.

~

The greatest beauty of all was the freedom from things—to clean, to look after, to fix, to buy. And the enormous sense of independence that we felt fishing and foraging—we learned to broil fish wrapped in kelp, to cook oysters in their shell on the coals, to boil water by dropping a hot rock in a mug, and to make salad from wild peas, wild mint, and sea asparagus. All that gave us the sense that, if we weren't invincible, then at least, if need be, we could manage on our own.

Except the wine.

~

After that summer, I began to understand Tuscans—their calm, their friendliness, their patience and ready smile. Why should they be any different? For thousands of years they have looked after themselves, each family in its fields and woods, surviving by their wits and hands. And, as Ofelio said as he planted his garlic last November when the world economy teetered on the brink, "Francesco, what's it matter? We have a house, a garden, chickens, two pigs, and cellar full of wine. They can roll up the roads and turn off the power; I'll happily go back tomorrow at least a hundred years." Then a smile broke on his face. "Then we can go hunting for hare every night."

9 ~ *TRUE SECURITY*
IN THE COUNTRY

*O*ld Tuscan front doors didn't have a handle (too complicated an affair—they liked to keep things simple). They did, of course, have a lock with a big chunky key; the only problem was that to keep the door from swinging open and letting in drafts, birds, and half the barnyard, you had to turn the key and lock yourself out of your own house. Since keys were expensive, being handmade by blacksmiths, and since most houses had a dozen or more habitants, from mom and pop and kids to grandparents, aunts, uncles, cousins, and whoever the dog had dragged in the day before, the safest solution to a) making sure the key was never lost and b) assuring everyone could get in at all times was to keep the key in the most secure place—the lock.

This tradition still persists; from dawn until bedtime our front door key rests where the blacksmith had meant it to be.

We have learned to apply the same notion to our cars; the most practical place to keep the key is in the ignition.

This has added many years to our lives, for police records show that ninety-nine percent of interfamily homicides begin with the loudly-screamed phrase, "Where's the fucken' key?!"

This unlocked door is not an end in itself but certainly a symptom of just how relaxing and safe life is in Tuscany. The reasons for the low crime rate is manyfold. First, there is a broad wellbeing with no desperate poverty, meaning you already own all the junk you want, so why would you go and bother stealing more? Second, we're too far from urban slums like Rome's (the trip is time-consuming, gas is eight dollars a gallon, and while the train is comfortable and the views pleasant, once you arrive you'd have to rent a car; so any thief with a decent business plan simply would not invest in such high upfront expense). Third, Tuscans live an unostentatious life, so most houses have little of value to steal, unless you have a fetish for self-lubricating tractors or sensor-activated hydro-pivot plows.

~

So it's easy to feel safe and secure in your house and neighborhood, but then the question of how to keep from starving to death arises, so you'll be alive to feel safe and secure tomorrow. But before we look at how to make a living in small towns and the country, perhaps it is best to examine the urban alternative first.

The Myth of the Steady Job

*And I fell to thinking of my silent, backstreet, basement office,
with its obliterated plate, rest-couch and velvet hangings, and
what it means to be buried there alive, if only from nine to five,
with convenient to one hand a bottle of light pale ale and to the
other a long ice-cold filet of hake. Nothing, I said, not even fully
certified death, can ever take the place of that.*
—Samuel Beckett, *All That Fall*

One of the advantages of urban and suburban life has been
the availability of that answer to all problems, the "Steady
Job."

Just how untrustworthy that term has turned out to be
is exemplified generally by the seven million jobs lost in this
recession, and specifically by the following from an article in
The New York Times.

"New Franklin, Ohio. It has been 10 months since
most of the workers walked out of the plain, low-slung factory here for the last time. The building, which has been
home to the Manchester Tool Company since just after
World War II, sits dormant now, a "for sale" sign buried in a
recent snowfall. The fallout of the plant's closure continues to
weigh heavily on the lives of the roughly 100 employees who
lost their livelihoods . . . less than 15% had a steady job
almost a year later. Many are sliding perilously close to the
economic precipice. Some let their health insurance lapse;
others are in danger of losing their modest homes. A similar

experience—or worse—may lie ahead for the hundreds of thousands of Americans who continue to lose their jobs every month. Many of the older hourly workers appear paralyzed . . . The machines they worked at Manchester tended to be specific to that plant and the skills to run them were not necessarily transferable."

By and large a Steady Job has turned out to be an illusion, yet for that part of us that has a dire need to believe in something constant, the Steady Job is right up there with Santa and the Easter Bunny. And why not? It sounds easy (most jobs are) and lucrative, and it promises not only a life of thought-free bliss, but also all the wonders of the mall.

And yet the worst of the myth is not that it misleads—it is only steady until you are laid off—but that it excludes, by preempting the option to lead an independent, varied, and truly secure life. Still, the Steady Job is such a lifeblood of our system that we manipulate our children toward it from an early age. The push for a career path from middle school onward is relentless to the almost complete exclusion of anything else.

So instead of working to fulfill our genetic desire for security, love, and friendship by building ourselves a home (one of the easiest jobs around), getting by, finding a lover and few good friends, and concentrating on becoming the wisest, kindest, wittiest, most creative human beings we can be, we pour our time and energy into training for, finding, and clutching a Steady Job. This is not only putting the cart before the horse, it's really more like putting it right on top of her.

~

We go on deluding ourselves that the horrendous recession of 2008-9 is just an aberration, ignoring that the whole last century was a cycle of boom and bust, of depression, war, recession, downsizing, bubble bursting, then again more recession. Even in normal times like 1970 to 1990, wages adjusted for inflation fell 20 percent. And while combined family income did climb a paltry 1 percent, not only has the average work week lengthened by 8 percent, but there are 40 percent more married women working.

Of course there were things to rejoice about—between 1970 and 1990 the number of Americans with yearly incomes of a million dollars or more increased from 642 to 62,000. Now, doesn't that make you feel a whole lot better?

There were some devastating days in the early nineties that taught us all cruel lessons in reality: Xerox announced a 20 percent trim of white collar jobs; Sears Roebuck eliminated 33,000 jobs; IBM let go 20,000 in addition to the 65,000 positions it had eliminated since 1986; banks and savings and loans slashed 50,000 jobs in one year; and instead of the annual bonus General Motors announced on December 18, 1991 the permanent termination of 70,000 long-standing jobs. One laid-off vice president, whose banker wife was also getting the ax, summed up the stunned reaction of the country in *The Times:* "Can you believe it? We both got into this thinking we were set for life."

Yet what is often more damaging than the paralysis and

loss of self esteem felt by the fallen Manchester Tool people, is the anxiety and stress suffered by those still standing. In emotional terms, being laid off is only slightly worse than the nagging dread that you'll be next to go. I remember our first years in Canada, when my stepfather, who had been a landscape architect in Hungary, was forced from job to menial job.

In those years the family worried and fought—about whether to buy meat, and who left the door open and let out costly heat, and how will we bear the shame when the neighbors see the re-possessors haul the couch and TV down the steps. And between the fights there was the silent shame on my stepfather's face because he, an intelligent, educated man, no matter how hard he worked, no matter how hard he tried, had somehow failed; was unable to guarantee his family a secure life.

The re-possessor never came—my mother paid the bills by cleaning people's houses—but for how bad we felt throughout those long winters, they might as well have come and carted off the lot.

As Louis Bromfield so wisely observed, "The high standard of living in America is an illusion based upon credit and the installment plan, which throw a man and his family into the street and on public relief the moment the factory closes and he loses his job."

And what's even more worrisome was the conclusion drawn by Andrew Stern, the president of the Service Employees International union, when over 650,000 jobs were lost in March of 2009: "There is something wrong with the system right now and we can't just say, 'Well, it's all going to work out.' It's not."

~

George Packer wrote in *The New Yorker* about Florida, "The Ponzi State," after the nearly apocalyptic housing market collapse in 2008. He described one of its innocent victims, Dan Hartzell, in his thirties, a hard worker with a wife and two children, laid off almost a year ago without explanation from a ten-dollar-an-hour job laminating plastic food bags in Tampa, Florida. He had been looking for work ever since— Home Depot, Sam's Club, Publix, at least sixty applications with no result. "You almost get to the point, where, what's the point . . . I start to wonder, what's wrong with me? Why do all these people view me as a bad person?" They were good, honest people, who never took out a subprime mortgage, hadn't lived beyond their means, but were now facing the real possibility of homelessness.

How can this be called a culture? A society? That leaves its hardest-working citizens homeless, riddled with self-doubt and such low self esteem? While the top one percent, who were the most active in fanning the flames of mindless profligacy are ferreting away millions? I'm sorry if I sound melodramatic, but the idea of a family without a roof over its heads just wrenches me with both anger and sorrow.

~

We seem to be caught on a runaway train of a system that anthropologist Colin Turnbull described as one of "cutthroat economics, where almost any kind of exploitation and degradation of others, impoverishment and ruin is justified in terms of an expanding economy and the consequent confinement of the world's riches in the pockets of the few."

Packer closes his article with a chillingly calm conclusion about Florida, America's dream, where not long ago a thousand new people arrived full of hope *every day.* "Florida holds up to the rest of the country a funhouse mirror of distorting accuracy . . . In a place like Lehigh Acres near Fort Meyers, where half the driveways are sprouting weeds, and where garbage piles up in the bushes along the outer streets, it's already possible to see the slums of the future. The vacant houses will be boarded up. The grass in the front yards will grow three feet high. The open fields with streetlights but no houses will become dumps."

Might be a good time to learn from Tuscany.

~

By its very nature, country living helps you avoid many traumas associated with the Steady Job. Its focus on multiple skills and flexibility and, most importantly, both physical and emotional survival methods, may not eliminate but will certainly dampen the shock of hard times. First of all, in the country you will most likely be self-employed, and hence unlikely—unless you're severely self-abusive—to be fired.

Secondly, if one of your skills becomes less in demand,

you can always hone up on or invent another.

But before we look at how you will earn money, be assured that, compared to your urban alter ego, you will need much less for house, car, clothes, food, and even entertainment.

The House

The most obvious saving will come from your house, whose price in the country will be miniscule compared to any home in a livable city. A house that would cost you a million dollars in Brooklyn would cost you one-tenth of that, with a half acre of land, in Duffy, NY, just 150 miles north of the Brooklyn Bridge. And for the price of a tiny studio in Rome you can have an old stone house on five acres in Tuscany.

The second best part is that while your home in the city is most often pure expense, in the country it can actually earn you money—in other words, your home itself can be a source of income. The most obvious and entertaining usage is that of a bed and breakfast. More and more travelers wisely choose the often stunning setting, the peace and quiet, and not to mention the homey feeling of sharing someone's house and being treated like visiting family—with the priceless advantage of not having to invite the people back. The best place to stay anywhere near us is the Girardi's six-room bed and breakfast with pool, excellent wine, and breakfasts fit for a king. The best place I've stayed in the U.S.—the most spoiling and charming, with the funniest, friendliest hosts, and fresh-squeezed juices, homemade marmalade, and French toast and poached eggs to die for—was Timbercliffe Cottage outside Camden, Maine. The most hilarious one was in the west of Ireland, where the most pious lady of the house kept Madonnas everywhere and a rosary and bible by each bedside, but once she saw all her guests tucked in for the night, out she'd go to have a "couple of pints." Then she'd return in the wee hours, softly singing and cursing her bloody key for being unable to find the hole in the bloody lock.

~

It's estimated that 7% of the U.S. labor force is involved in telecommuting; that is, having transferred an office job to their home. With powerful computers, broadband, and video conferences, physical presence is of diminishing value when it comes to conducting business. It's a blessed far cry from twenty years ago, when we moved into our first Tuscan house without even a phone, and Bazzotti, at whose house the telephone line ended, had to ring an old cow bell when we got calls from New York or send his daughter Alessandra running down the road, yelling, *"Vieni, vieni, C'è Il Libro del Mese al telefono."* It took me the whole breathless run uphill to figure out we had a call from our editor with an Italian dictionary at Book of the Month.

And don't think you have to work for yourself to relocate to the country; many corporations, realizing the savings in office space and accompanying overhead, would happily have you work out of your home—which led a friend at a

New York magazine to remark, "Pretty soon the only one left here will be the receptionist to tell whoever comes that everyone is gone."

The Professions

With modern technology, many a country professional can work from home: lawyers, accountants, and architects, not to mention psychologists, chiropractors, fortune tellers, and morticians (although the latter would have to invest in a bigger fridge). A friend, a geothermal expert who travels the world, keeps his home base in his house in Tuscany; another started a hot air balloon service; and of course you can start another Apple Computers, given the right garage.

The Crafts

Fine craftsman work is experiencing a renaissance worldwide, and there is no better place for the cottage craft industry than the country. Everything from small boat building to jewelry and one-off designer clothing is booming like never before. In New York, everyone from Bergdorf to Barney's is looking for something unique and lasting. Here in Tuscany, there is no end to country art. A leathersmith thrives in Pienza, and two potters do well in small shops in Montalcino, as does a weaver whose ware amazed a friend who designs for Moschino. The most beautiful jewelry, based on Etruscan goldsmithing and designs, comes out of a husband-and-wife studio in Montepulciano. Nearby, Chianciano has a small bindery specializing in leather covers for old and new books alike. A friend makes fabulously creative hats for boutiques in Rome, and a local woodworker makes bowls and kitchen tools out of fascinatingly grained olive. Then there is the Biagiotti family of blacksmiths in Pienza, who make wrought iron everything, from tables and chairs to beds and candelabras, and of course every town has its own furniture maker and refinisher.

Now, the vital thing that sets apart most Tuscan crafts from their North American counterparts, is a simple word: practicality. Whereas we're used to arts and crafts meaning "gifty" items, the Tuscan version refers to everyday, useful things like tables, chairs, curtains, bags, and clothes. The only way they differ from their off-the-rack cousins is that they are most often unique, beautiful, and of such superb quality that they last for life.

With people reevaluating their lives in the aftermath of such economic turmoil, the swing from quantity to quality is well underway on both sides of the Atlantic. Claire Cain Miller wrote in *The New York Times* that "on Sept 29, 2008, a day the stock market plunged sharply, Etsy, the leading Web marketplace for hand-made goods, had record sales. And in November and December the site has continued to break records. Last month artists sold $10.8 million of goods on Etsy, more than double the year before. Some merchants had such unexpectedly high sales they had to shut down early because they do not have time to produce anymore." Apart from the lower costs, handmade goods have a non-financial value that appeals to many buyers. As one lady said, "'I just like the fact that I'm supporting someone who's trying to make their way in the world by using their talents, and my money is going directly to a person instead of a chain of middlemen.'"

~

I can attest that there are few things as precious as those made by an artisan, whose heart and soul goes into his work. I bought a travel bag from a young leathersmith in Laguna Beach 38 years ago. It was of sturdy but beautifully-tanned hide, hand stitched, intelligently thought-out pockets all around. The bag has been with me in over 40 countries, on freighters, helicopters, sailboats, canoes, and mule back, thrashed, thrown, run over, and beaten, and it's just as solid as the day it was made, and even more beautiful with some patina from wear. And if I ever had to give up all my wordly goods, that leather bag would be the last to go.

~

And if you personally know the craftsman, the greater the attachment still. A visit to the goldsmiths in Montepulciano is visiting old friends. Not only do they know what I like to get for Candace, but they create things unasked, like lapis lazuli earrings to match a necklace I'd bought her one

Christmas years before.

And there is no gift more special than one made just for you. Vi Smith, who lives on a small peninsula across from our desert island, spins and dyes her own wool. She knit a sweater for Buster when he was five. Over the heart was a little lamb made of raw wool in bas-relief. He cherished that sweater and wore it for years, well beyond the point that it still fit him. It is now safely put away, awaiting his own child.

~

Some fear isolation when working a craft, but with a little invention and some skill, you can form partnerships.

Thirty years ago, scattered in hamlets around Montalcino, were five classic cabinet makers who could take a rough-hewn board and, with the simplest hand tools, create masterpieces of furniture as well as the unique doors and windows of all curvatures and sizes that the ancient buildings and medieval houses need. But with the advent of large factories using aluminum, it became cheaper to alter the opening than to buy a hand-made door. The demand for their work began to slow. One day, one of them, Renaldo, always enthusiastic, suggested they join forces and create an enterprise. Ugo, always pensive, had his doubts. He quoted a Tuscan proverb, *"Se mi metto a fare il cappellaio, nasce la gente senza testa."* If I become a hat-maker, people will be born without heads.

But Renaldo won out.

The five craftsmen formed a cooperative called Arte 5.

They invested in equipment that enabled them to make one-of-a-kind doors and windows with the aid of a computerized machine. They became the new craftsman, making hand-made masterworks with the latest technology.

The Craftsmen of Food

If there is a single person revered in Montalcino—apart from the elegant octogenarian Franco Biondi-Santi, standard-bear-er of the family who invented Brunello—it has to be Giovanna, our baker. She is short and powerful, a typical Tuscan lady with a ready smile but the discipline of a gener-al. Her family has been baking since 1892 in the small bak-ery in the narrowest part of our main street. Her miniscule store is usually deep in people awaiting their turn, inhaling the fragrance of the still-warm breads: pane *integrale* (whole wheat) or *ciambella* (like a giant doughnut), *ciabatta* (slipper, because it's flat) or the normal, hard-crusted Tuscan bread. She also bakes *focaccia*, two *crostatas*—one with plum jam, the other with apricot—a great *mille foglie*, and for the day of the dead, *Pane dei Santi* (a heavy loaf of nuts and raisins), and for *carnevale*, *crogetti* (deep-fried and drenched in honey).

Few things make me as happy—or as hungry—as start-ing up the cobblestone hill toward Giovanna's.

We have two revered butchers who not only make spectacular *prosciutto*s, sausages, and salamis, but also raise their own pigs to get the best quality meats possible. And we have more than a dozen bee-keepers in our valley making exotic wild honeys. One shop makes sinfully good chocolates and pastries, two shops make their own gelato, and of course two tiny pizzerias sell fresh pizza by the slice. And there is a family of fishermen who, on Tuesday and Friday mornings, open up a little shop and fill it with fresh fish.

In a nearby town a shop that makes and sells only fresh pasta. The Cugusi family in Montepulciano produces amazing pecorino, sheep cheeses, some as tasty but less sweet than *parmigiano*. One store in Pienza specializes in wild boar, another in homemade jams.

Oh yes, I almost forgot: there's two hundred of us crazy families making Brunello, most of whom started as *"garagistes,"* fermenting in places literally the size of a garage.

Then there are those who grow fruits and vegetables, raise poultry and eggs, and bring them to market once a week, while some do as Vi Smith does on Pender Island, leaving garden produce on a table by the gate, and you take what you want and leave your money in a jar. If that peaceful thought doesn't make you take a deep sigh, then have a glass of wine, because you're running on empty.

~

With any craft, whether of food or wares, you will surely work long hours, but at least you'll sleep well at night, knowing you're producing something as good as your hands—and mind—can make.

And none of these crafts will ever make you rich, but then what exactly has that to do with life?

Etcetera

In urban and suburban life, our cars have to be both flashy and new, lest the neighbors mistake us for the cleaning lady or gardener. In the country, a beat-up pickup is the epitome of fashion. Despite the fact that country roads inflict wear and tear, cars are kept at least a decade—our Civic is in its eleventh year. With the savings on payments, maintenance, insurance, and depreciation, driving a country car can save you a bundle.

Urban life means lots of clothes, for most of us would rather go naked than wear the same thing two days in a row. And our clothes, like our cars, are discarded not because they are worn out, but because they have simply gone out of some laughable thing called fashion.

In the country, clothes live on and on. I just retired a waxed jacket I bought in Ireland twenty-six years ago because there were more holes than material left, and I still wear an Irish sweater and a French fisherman's sweater, both of which I've had for over thirty years.

As for food in the country, even for those who don't grow or raise their own, the savings are beyond compare. Buying direct from farms leaves out the middlemen. And buying in bulk, often by the sack, costs a fraction of what you'd pay out in the city. Friends often buy whole calves or pigs and divide it up, not just saving a bundle, but also guaranteeing that they get free-range animals raised without hormones and antibiotics.

~

As for the rest? In urban and suburban life, much of our income is spent going out to overcome the hollow feeling of being alone in a crowd. And every time we step out the door, we pay. We spend vast sums on gyms, manicures, and expensive dinners just to show ourselves why we work so hard. And the nearly universal cure for urban and suburban depression is to shop. Instead, in the country, you can go chop some wood, or go for a walk in the sunshine or the moonlight, and you'll feel like a million bucks without spending a dime.

Social life in the country seems much more intense than its urban counterpart. A good example might be our first year in Whistler, where the sun went down early and brought long winter nights.

The roads were treacherous all winter. Travel at night was hard, and there was nowhere to go but the local pub, or for a walk in the moonlit snow. The second week we were there, someone had the idea to start a theater. Live. Our own. So we started one in the old schoolhouse, ten of us, all adults, with almost no experience, and no stage, no sets, no lights—and we did plays by Beckett, Pinter, Shaw, and Edward Albee. I had taken some theater at university so I knew a bit about acting and directing, but the rest of the people didn't have a clue, and didn't really care. They weren't there to become stars, they were there to have some fun.

Everyone seemed to instantly shed inhibitions or pretensions, and we roared with laughter at the audacious gestures each of us invented, and at intonations no one dreamed of and often wished they'd never made.

The best part was that all of us, most of whom had hardly known each other, became instant friends. And with one couple we remained best friends for life. That rarely happens when you go out to a movie.

And as much as I loved living in New York and as much as I love theater from Lincoln Center to Lower East Side basements, I must say that those snowy nights were as vibrant and full of life as any play I can remember.

The difference must be between "fun" and "entertainment." One is a passionate living of your life; the other is watching someone do it for you.

~

Here in Tuscany, nights out mean to the house of friends, who, in the country, become much more precious. And each gathering means not just a shared closeness but a memorable feast of great food and wine. Then there are neighbors. Nothing beats walking to the Paoluccis' and sitting around the fire watching Nonna sew, or Franco weave a new basket for picking olives, sipping wine while talking about the farm, the fruit trees, the vines, and who was born, got engaged, got married, or died, the memories, the loss, things that were near to you, dear to you. And you walk home feeling the wine, on the dark dirt road that winds under the stars, and sense some kind of contact with it all—the friends, the silent valley, the animals in the stalls, the bracing chill of winter or the warmth of a summer night. You feel that you belong.

~

As for vacations, I cannot tell you how many times we had planned, made reservations, even sent deposits, yet so many times—unless it was a unique place like the Seychelles or Andalusia or Pelopenes—spots of remarkable history or beauty—we, at the last minute, looked at our house and the countryside around us and decided the best place was, as always has been, home.

10 ~ THE NEW/OLD
FAMILY FARM

It seemed to me that real continuity, real love of one's country, real permanence, had to do not with mechanical inventions and high wages but with the earth and man's love of the soil upon which he lived.

—Louis Bromfield, *At Malabar*

*A*t the beginning of the thirteenth century, the Tuscan countryside came alive. Earlier, fears of marauders had kept citizens living inside fortressed towns, venturing out during the day to let animals graze while they worked the land but retreating back inside the security of the walls when evening fell. With the newfound peace between city-states—Florence not yet powerful enough and Siena not yet ambitious enough—the citizens began to emigrate to the country, and that fabled structure, the Tuscan country house, began to take shape.

"It is truly beautiful to contemplate the infinite multitude of houses which populate the hills," wrote Montaigne in 1581 from the top of Giotto's tower in the heart of Florence. He was commenting on the most visually evident form of country life: the villas and farm houses of an existence which for centuries had formed among *padroni e contadini*, landowners and farmers.

The houses themselves, which were of almost "mythic nature," he went on, "cosmic, perennial, hence classic, wear still and forever a character, an aspect of almost religious piety.

"There is a common element to all this architecture, that never distances itself from common sense, almost musical in proportions, without impulsive outbursts or caprice; all eddies of purity, tranquil harmony, and above all a sense of measure, of serenity. It is a fragment of a world perfect in itself, enclosed, complete, where is gathered all that is necessary for the health of life: the house, the fields, the vegetable gardens, the other products of the land, the wild fragrances of woods and flowers, the diverse voices of animals, the hills, and beyond all that, the infinite, mystery which one contemplates from here persuaded of the great truth that all comes from the land and to the land all returns."

The Classic Tuscan Farm

La Pieve di Santa Restituta, the country church you pass before our house, was first mentioned in the history books in the seventh century. It was built beside a Roman road that lead from the malaria swamps of the coast inland through the hills. Pilgrims stopped here on the way to Rome, and one of them, Charlemagne, founded a church in a tranquil dale one hill to the east.

When we bought Il Colombaio, it was an abandoned ruin. The fields were overgrown, bramble covered the olives, the old vineyard had been flattened by wind and rain, and the Mediterranean forests were tangled by windfall. Yet, there was a voice, beyond all reason, that said, "This is good."

The only sign of life left behind were some barrels with rusted staves, a plow, some hand-blown demijohns, and, in the guard tower, a pile of papers: books, maps, letters, documents. The most fascinating thing was a map, badly stained, that showed a dozen farmhouses in our valley, demarcating all fields and woods and indicating by symbols what was planted where.

The shapes of the fields and the houses varied somewhat, but overall the feeling of each *podere* was the same: each seemed to be its own self-contained kingdom.

A house, surrounded by its walled barnyard, was usually set near the road to be accessible and sociable. The fields next to the house were planted in grain, with trees evenly planted within a short walk of one another, close enough to reach shade for a rest from the heat, a bite, and a slug of wine. Rows of vines were interrupted by fruit trees and olives. By alternating grains, legumes, and forage, not only was the soil always replenished, but the mixed plants gave habitats to a variety of insects that kept each other in check. Next to the fields, each *podere* had classic forests, the woodlot.

Until fifty years ago, vast tracts of land, with great numbers of *poderes*, belonged to single families, yet the owners found it more sustainable, more productive, and more human to give independence to each house, giving each family room for livestock, poultry, grain, olive oil, wood, pasture, and wine—everything needed to sustain a well-lived life.

~

But the food and wine a Tuscan farm yields is only a small portion of what the land truly bequeaths. The work it requires is both demanding and robust, and in return it yields a physically active and thus healthy life. On a farm of such great variety, you are in constant motion. Admittedly, some days, like those spent hauling wood from the canyon, are back-breaking and bruising, but it's a chance to test your strength, build some muscle, get a few nicks and sprains, and feel alive. And you'll experience an arousing physical exhilaration that could never be duplicated in normal urban life, unless you were to hire someone to beat you with a two-by-four.

Judging by our neighbors far into their seventies and some in their eighties, this naturally active life keeps you healthy and alert far into your years. Settimia finally slowed down when she fell off a ladder picking olives. She was eighty-five.

Castelli is even older, but he still commands his wine estate and is so agile and quick, he might just outrun the hearse taking him to his grave.

~

The mental exercise a farm provides is pretty much the same. While some work is repetitious, with the great variety of things planted and animals tended, choices and judgments seldom are: you have to adjust to weather, needs, urgency, and mood, so the freshness seldom wanes. Take one of the simplest tasks: pruning vines. On each vine, you have to cut away the dead wood of the year before, and you must leave only four or five shoots—the rest have to go. The ones you leave should be evenly spaced, and not growing out of some very old spur or growing downward, where it's more likely to break. Once you've chosen the five, you must cut as close to the cordon—the bent horizontal part—as possible, but you must leave on each two tiny, unopened "eyes," future buds, and the "*lupo*," wolf, an even smaller eye down in the crotch of the shoot, so it will survive a late frost or hail that could lay waste to the other two, above. So now you cut the old shoot past the top bud but not just any old way; you cut it sloping away from the top eye so rainwater runs off and not onto the eye, where it could settle and freeze on a frosty night. And all the while you must keep up your part in the endless vineyard chatter. See what I mean by "mental excercise?"

~

Not long ago, the farmer and his wife were the most diverse

and inventive people in the land. They had to know more about more things than anyone in another profession. The farmer had to be a botanist, biologist, carpenter, mechanic, veterinarian, midwife, weather forecaster, and tireless digger of the soil. The farm wife was a horticulturist, animal handler, culinary wizard, food-preserving expert, accountant, and confessor, who sat with endless patience and heard her husband's woes. And they both had to have the calm of a philosopher and the patience of a saint to survive all the adversities man and God heaped on them. Almost as important, they had to be first-class human beings and even better friends, for on farms of old everyone needed the help of his neighbor to survive. And most farmers were all that and more. As Louis Bromfield wrote in the late 1930s, "For companionship, good conversation, intelligence and the power of stimulating one's mind, there are none I would place above a good farmer."

A Tuscan Family Farm

The best example I know of small-scale farming is the farm of the Paoluccis. Their valley is one of the most beautiful in Tuscany. It was once ocean bottom—with almost every shovelful you dig up a fossil—so the hills are softly rounded, gently rolling, reflecting the endless motion of the sea, the flowing of the tides, the sculpting of the currents. In early summer, when the wheat is green and the winds blow hard, the hills and valleys ripple like an ocean.

The Paoluccis' house sits on a narrow clay road that runs along a ridge in the middle of the valley. When I say narrow, I mean if two cars meet on the road, one has to back up to let the other pass. And when I say "on the road," I mean you have to take care the hay cart doesn't knock a cornerstone from the wall of the house. This to us North Americans might seem a strange location for a house, for we like to be far from roads and other people to escape noise and unwanted eyes. But the Italian countryside is quiet, and the neighbors constitute much of the social life. For a neighbor to pass by without stopping for a word would be almost like a slap in the face.

The Paoluccis' seven hectares—about seventeen acres—straddle the road. The fields are of various shapes and sizes, with more types of crops than you can count on both your hands. The biggest single crop is seven acres of grain, mostly wheat, rotating sometimes with oats and sometimes with alfalfa to replenish the soil. Some of the wheat is fine-milled for pasta and bread for the family, some coarse-milled for the pigs, cows, chickens, ducks, and uncountable other fowl, and the rest, about five tons, is sold. After the grain fields, the next biggest produce hay to feed the cows and rabbits; then come the small fields, the true treasures of the farm, which yield the most valuable crops.

No one is sure how many acres the vineyard takes up, because there are three *vigna*s of rather bizarre shapes, but there are 2,500 grapevines altogether, yielding an annual harvest of near 10,000 pounds of grapes. A quarter is made into wine for the family, some sold direct in demijohns or bottles, while the rest is sold fresh to large *cantinas*, who buy grapes from different growers to make wine. The vineyard income varies, depending on how much is sold and how. If you take the time to turn the grape to wine yourself, you can sell it *sfuso*, or in bulk, for about twice the price.

Even more treasured than vineyards are olive groves. Tuscan olive oil is flavorful, pungent, and sought after and it sells for $20 a kilo, about $10 a pound, direct from the farm. No farmhouse would be complete without a year's supply safely in the cantina in clay jars, and few things are valued more highly than your own olive orchard. Growing olives is a farmer's dream. You prune but once every two years, plow the grove only once a year, spread manure from the stalls once, and while it is true that the harvesting is slow—olive by olive, all by hand—an old tree can yield up to forty kilos of oil, and that's a lot.

But the mainstays at the Paoluccis are the various animals they raise around the house. From the litters of two pigs, they keep two or three piglets for themselves; the rest they raise for two to three months, then they sell them off at market. But the most highly sought-after meat is milk-fed veal. Paolucci usually has three calves at a time, and he can normally sell them at four months. The Paoluccis also sell dressed chickens and rabbits to people who come from town, and the chickens lay about a dozen eggs a day, some of which get sold off, the rest kept to nourish the family.

The rest of their food comes from their vast vegetable

garden. It is spread out in three places on the farm.

Fruit trees are everywhere. *Susina*, a smallish local plum, grows wild here and is used for jams, preserves, and baking. Peaches, pears, cherries, and apricots yield small crops in the hard clay, but their flavors are the envy of Italy. What the Paoluccis don't eat in the summer they preserve for winter. Tomatoes are either stewed or sun-dried, artichokes are kept in oil, and all fruits are canned.

The great fireplace in the kitchen heats the house in winter. Fires in the woodstove all year round make those wonderful roast ducks, roast rabbits, and roast pigeons. The wood for both of these Paolucci cuts in a forest two miles up the valley, hauling it home behind the tractor on a cart.

The Paoluccis' farm is as un-mechanized as a modern farm can get. There is only one tractor, twenty years old, that is used about 150 hours a year for everything from plowing to hauling hay, wood, grapes, or casks of wine. They also have a small machine for cutting hay, and they have a car, a little Fiat, and an Ape, a three-wheeled truck that's really a 100 cc motorbike with sheet metal wrapped around it and a small flatbed behind. And a bicycle.

Their farm needs little from outside sources. They feed the animals only what they grow, and, in return, the animals provide manure for the crops. The Paoluccis produce almost no garbage and no waste. Their self-reliance is profound, and they eat better food—fresher, more nourishing, more flavorful—than any king.

It is true the hours are long. The day starts at 6:30 a.m.,

with the feeding of the animals, and ends around 6:00 p.m. in summer and about 4:00 p.m. in winter—with those memorable five-course lunches in between. But what never seems to change at the Paoluccis, regardless of the season, what has always seemed remarkable to me, is the pace. Franco never hurries. When I help him with the hay, or the *vendemmia*, or the olives, the phrase I most often hear is *"Piano—piano"*, which means, "Slowly—slowly."

This is the sign of neither laziness nor a lack of strength. The man has muscles like rocks, and he works every day but Sunday. But there exists an inimitable leisure in his life, something tranquil, a kind of peace, as if he always were—which he always is—at home. And I'm not talking about some pious holy man, but a devout Tuscan who will swear at the top of his lungs in the house or in the fields, who will laugh uproariously or howl in blazing fury—but around this boisterous life, or more correctly, under it, is a serene lake of contentment, the joy of being alive. He is unhurried because each moment is good; he doesn't need to rush to get to something better.

So Paolucci lives and works *piano—piano.* He gathers clover for the rabbits and stops for a chat, or to watch the birds, or he walks down to the pond to see the ducks or sits for a while on his worn stone steps and tilts the two-liter bottle of wine that's always there, and pours himself a glass.

But to pretend that farm work is all strolling and picking daisies would be lying. Franco's wife has shoulders broader than mine, and Nonna, who turned 80 last year, has strength from a life of labor that lets her throw a bale of hay up on the cart with me still hooked onto it, and Paolucci's hands are gnarled and craggy from the dry clay sucking at them. To pretend that the farm is heaven would be leaving out shoveling pig shit and cow shit, and sitting on the open tractor in the blazing sun, and loading those cursed bales of hay in sizzling July. It would be to leave out the fear of drought year after year, the fear of rain, the worry about animal health, insects, molds, and foxes. But, rising every morning on a farm instead of in an artificial suburb or a cell of an apartment, and seeing the sun rise over hills and trees instead of behind concrete towers; walking to the barn on a silent, dusty road sparkling with dew instead of driving bumper-to-bumper on some endless freeway; smelling the fresh dawn and the live barn instead of smog and fumes; looking up and seeing sky instead of ceiling tiles; spending the day roaming the hills under the sun and filling your lungs with clean oxygen with every breath instead of being shut in a box breathing recycled air; compared to that relentless half-life in the city, shoveling pig shit is truly paradise.

A New England Farm

The tiny village of Jackson straddles the Wildcat River, just below Jackson Falls, in the White Mountains of New Hampshire. You approach it on curvy mountain roads. In the winter, you wind among snow-draped forests and streams so thick with ice that the surging water breaks through only now and then.

On one side of the river, the bay-windowed hotel dates from 1869, the church, with its open belfry and white steeple, from 1847, and the squat library, like a fanciful old barn, from the turn of the century. Across the bridge are scattered the post office, two eateries, some shops, and the Jackson Grammar School, as pretty a New England clapboarder as you have seen.

The land in these parts is not a farmer's dream. The latitude is high, the winter long—apple trees seldom blossom before Memorial Day. The terrain is hilly and tiring, and the soil is so rocky that a tractor has to plow one furrow at a time instead of the four or five it could in decent soil. In the winter the winds are foul. Atop Mount Washington, a few miles north of town, the wind often reaches eighty miles an hour, bringing the wind-chill factor to minus 100 degrees Fahrenheit, below which no one has ever bothered to keep score.

The Davis family has farmed the same piece of land here for nine generations.

Two miles north of Jackson, at the foot of Black Mountain, they live on a sprawling farm of 320 acres. Half of it is fields and open pasture, the other half a forest of sugar maple, birch, ash, and, in the higher portions, clusters of fir and pine. Bob Davis, his wife Bea, and one of their three sons live in the big frame house built by his great-great-grandfather in 1863. The wood barn, with its foundation of dry-laid fieldstone, was put up the same year.

Forty years ago, these hills were all worked by families like the Davises, most of them with less land, but all of them engaged, like the Davises, in widely mixed farming—sugaring the maple forest in the winter, growing corn, raising cattle, pigs, and poultry for meat, running dairies, and tending fields of pumpkins. As recently as the 1960s, between here and Conway, where the bottom land is more plentiful, there were twenty-five good-sized dairies, some running fifty milkers, some nearly 300. The valley has changed drastically since then. The dairies have closed down and the farms have been sold off piece by piece to weekenders from distant towns, who build condominiums and chalets. But Bob Davis and his family have stayed on.

Their farming now is more mixed than ever. With his two grown sons working with him, Bob Davis, now fifty-three years old, tall, gaunt, quiet, with a mind as quick and witty as you'll find anywhere, talks first about the livestock, which "we feed every morning before we feed ourselves." In the winter, that means mushing through the snow and darkness to a barn that's warm and humid from the bodies of the cattle, cutting open fresh bales of hay, and pitching them into the troughs or just in piles on the dirt floor. In the summer, the cows roam the pastures or the woods in search of exotic fodder. The Davises raise twenty-five head at a time now, half dairy cows that they raise from calves until they freshen (meaning that they can calve) at two-and-a-half years, and the other half for meat, slaughtering, dressing, and selling— usually by the side—to neighbors in the valley. The cattle weigh around 500 pounds when dressed. A half a cow they freeze, and that keeps them in beef for the year.

The fifty acres of hay that they cut yields 8,000 bales. Of this, their own cattle eat 3,000; the rest they sell in bales in the summer from the field, or in fall and winter from the barn. They have a hundred acres that's plain pasture, and since cattle don't need more than an acre a head, they take in cow boarders in the months the grass grows well. And they cultivate an acre of sweet corn and an acre of pumpkins, both of which they sell direct.

Then there are the chickens. Their numbers vary with the season, but there are normally twenty-five being raised as roasters or fryers, which they sell at eight weeks. They keep about sixty layers, which lay four dozen eggs a day. The eggs are set in cardboard cartons on the kitchen table—the door is always unlocked—and people come and help themselves and leave money in a cup.

From late spring on there is the vegetable garden. It is about forty by a hundred feet, on the flat top of a hill that gets the longest hours of sun. Here Bea grows everything— peas, beans, carrots, onions, broccoli—and what they don't eat fresh she freezes up, and they eat it through the winter.

They also keep two pigs, one to slaughter in the spring and one in the fall, for ham, pork chops, and bacon. So through the mild season the pantry builds up and the treasury builds up and, just as important, the spirit stays fresh because the work is always varied. There are different jobs, different seasons, in the fields, in the forest, in the barn, and, within limits, you are free to choose the chore that suits your mood. This variety is a boon not only to the spirit but also to the family's security. If any single crop fails, or livestock falters, there are other things to fall back on, unlike the single-crop large-scale farmer, whose single misfortune can lead to financial disaster.

In the winter the world changes on the Davis farm. The leaves are gone by late October and the cold winds from Canada begin blowing down the valley. The corn and the pumpkins have been picked and sold, and the vegetable garden is wilted and empty, save for the potatoes huddled underground. Bob Davis and his sons head up into the woods. There are always fallen trees from last winter's storms to be cleaned and cut with chainsaws, pulled down the hill by tractor, bucked, cut up, then, without splitting, laid up for a couple of years to dry. They need eight cords for themselves for the winter, but they don't stop there. Woods as large as theirs, carefully managed, can yield a lot of firewood and have for generations. So the Davises take as much as 150 cords every winter to lay up, while they pull out the seasoned wood, split it, and deliver it to the valley by the chord.

When the snow falls—nowadays much less frequently than before—they hook a snowplow on the tractor and plow the roads and driveways in the valley. Every bit helps. They don't get rich pushing snow around, but it helps them buy a better grade of machine, or better gear, and that can make a lot of difference on a farm.

Then there is the sugar orchard. There is a twenty-acre

orchard in the hills with 1,800 good-size sugar maples in it. For generations, sugaring was the year's highlight on the Davis farm, marking, as it always did, the end of the long winter. But the activity is not only to celebrate the approaching spring, not only to look forward to remuneration for their labor. It is one of the times of year when young and old work together, and the valley's kids all come just for the fun of trudging through the snow with flapping snowshoes, or driving the team of horses that pull the big wood sleigh, hauling the wooden tank sloshing full of sap, or spending hours by the blazing fire under the big iron evaporator in the sugar house feeding the roaring flames with three-foot hunks of wood, milling about in the great billows of steam that belch out of the shadows, bucketing in the sap and bucketing out the syrup, then slumping back into the snowy woods for more.

But sugaring is no frivolous party. You slump through the woods on snowshoes, a tiring chore even empty-handed, and you lurch from tree to tree with a pair of five-gallon tin buckets, filling them with sap. When the buckets are full and the snow soft, you sink in a good foot-and-a-half on every step, buckets, snowshoes, curses, and all; then, all out of breath, you yank your foot out and slump on and thank God for the horses because they came when you whistled and saved you a trip back. There is no time to waste; when the sap runs, you run.

But when things go well sugaring is a dream and the money is good. You haul a lot of sap—thirty to forty-five gallons of it for every precious gallon of sweet syrup at the end. There was a time when the Davis family bottled up to 400 gallons of syrup in a good year, and Bob's grandmother sold it all, one small jug at a time, by mail order, all over the country. Even now, when working fewer trees brings in much less syrup, the eighty dollars they get for each gallon helps to keep the family kitty just a little fatter.

~

It must be obvious by now that living off the land in northern New Hampshire is no permanent vacation. But I chose New Hampshire for just that reason, for if the Davises have managed in this changing, rocky place of long cold winters for nine generations, then one can certainly survive working the rich soils in the better climates of Virginia or Alberta or Oregon. But Bob Davis and his family have stayed because they like the silence, like the trees, like being their own bosses. The one thing that Bob Davis misses is the people, not the unknown masses that now amble every weekend through the towns, but the friends who have moved away. Sometimes he thinks of moving on to a less changed place, back among small farmers, back to where the neighbors are friends, like they were here forty years ago.

11 ~ THE TUSCAN
FOOD GARDEN

To forget to dig the earth and tend the soil is to forget ourselves.
—Mahatma Gandhi

The Tuscan family, in all its complexity and wide-ranging loyalty, is the foundation of Tuscany, but nearly as fundamental is the edible Tuscan garden. Even in our wine-producing zone, where affluent vintners are common, the most constant and beloved area is right around the house: the orchard, the olive grove, an enormous vegetable garden, and of course the barnyard, bristling with life—and it hasn't changed much over the centuries.

In a not-too-distant past, the same could have been said of many a family home in the western world, but something changed, and even modest vegetable gardens vanished and the fruit trees vanished, replaced by antiseptic lawns and a few shrubs. This is a most curious transition, especially because surveys show that gardening is most people's favorite pastime. Our friends in big cities, from New York to Milan, concur: their greatest weekend joy involves digging dirt. They seem to have some internal need that makes them go to extreme difficulties to have dirt to dig. A friend in Brooklyn hauled soil in buckets up to rooftop planters, where she planted herbs, tomatoes, radishes, and parsley. Another in Milan had a crane haul soil onto her roof, where, in raised beds of three hundred square feet, she has both summer and winter vegetables, enough to feed the neighbors in her building. And this has nothing to do with saving money on groceries. Two friends, both senior editors in New York City, with sufficient family funds to buy a medium-sized country, spend weekends growing so much food that they often come to work Monday mornings laden with bags of vegetables and pass them to everyone around the office.

I have always loved the idea of growing our own food, and admired Candace and Buster going at it with hoe and shovel, but I never quite understood the great visceral joy until Candace announced one evening that the moon was perfect for planting garlic but, since she was busy in the wine cellar, I had to go do it.

Now why a bloody clove of garlic stuck two inches underground would give a rat's ass about what the moon is doing ninety thousand miles above, I haven't a clue, but I've learned long ago that in Tuscany you don't doubt folklore, so out I went. Now, some people love baseball, others adore their cars, I love garlic. It was November, the sky clear, Venus blinding bright, and I quickly hoed and weeded a big patch, crumbled the soil, grooved in the rows, and then split the garlic heads up into cloves—on Candace's advice keeping only the biggest and the best, for the nourishment of the young plant comes from the clove itself. And pointy end up, she had said with a pained smile, as if she had already written off our garlic for next year.

I spaced them well, all hundred and twenty of them, shoved them an inch deep, and then lovingly covered them with another inch of soil. Then I watered them lightly because Candace had informed me that garlic isn't goldfish. For a week, nothing much happened. Then one came up. Then another. Then more, then every one. I have built sailboats and houses and written a dozen books, but I can honestly say I have never felt a more unbridled pride. Not because I had helped something to life, but because before me lay a near-jungle of garlic that would be rubbed onto our *bruschetta* with fresh olive oil, or chopped fine for the clam sauce that went over *linguini*, or arranged around the pork loin roasting by the fire. My garlic. My own handmade garlic. With a nudge from the moon.

At Colombaio, the food garden completely encircles the house. We transplanted a hundred olives in a ring, like a moat, enough to keep us and our best friends in olive oil through the year, then we planted fifty fruit trees of every kind, a field of artichokes, a huge strawberry patch, rows of asparagus, a field of spuds, a summer vegetable garden

breeze-cooled and in the shade, and a winter garden surrounded by stone walls to hold the heat. Above the house
under an old oak we found chanterelles that we now tend and
water and guard against the gourmet wild boar that try every
year to beat us to the punch.

And all year round we watch with anticipation as
things sprout and bloom to end up feeding us through the
year. To try to compare rationally anything you grew with
your own hands, that you planted, watered, nursed, protected from all evil, watched grow and ripen every day for weeks,
to try to compare that with any fruit or vegetable grown by
mere mortals elsewhere on this planet is a futile task: theirs
don't have a snowball's chance in hell. Yours, blemished,
dwarfed, misshapen as they may be, will be sweeter, richer,
have flavors never imagined, while theirs will be watery, taste-
less, barely edible pulp. I'm not exaggerating when I say that
I look forward all morning of each summer's day to the time
when, just before lunch, I go out to the garden and pick the
darkest, reddest tomatoes on the vines. To bite into a tomato
you grew yourself, fully ripe, gushing flavor and fragrance,
with the warmth of the sun still lingering in it—well, there is
nothing in the world that can taste so good. Except garlic.

And fresh peas rolling out of the shell as sweet as honey,
or radishes just uprooted and full of all the flavors they have
drawn out of the earth, or the apricots you have watched for
days waiting for that perfect, ripest moment—a moment
before the bloody birds come and eat the bloody lot—when
as you touch it, it tumbles into your palm, soft, full of nec-

tar, that first bite—well, it's worth waiting the whole year for.

This mania for homegrown food runs in the Tuscan's blood. Even those who live in towns have tiny plots nearby, with a little shed for tools and food gardens run amok. Monte Argentario was once an island now attached to the mainland by a sandy spit. The hills are dry, steep, and rocky, with old shepherds' and fishermen's houses now all summer homes. The land is so steep it had to be terraced. The views over the azure Tyrennian Sea and the islands of Giglio and Elba would make any weekender sit and stare in awe. But they don't. They get out their hoes and work that unforgiving soil around a few vines, olives, and fig trees, and in their shade they plant whatever vegetables they can eke out of the soil with rainwater they have collected in cisterns through the year.

And these Tuscan gardens don't just survive because Tuscans have a genetic need to hoe: if you ask anyone who works their bit of land, just the gleam in their eyes when they reply is enough to tell you why.

I asked Paolucci once, with the weekly market brimming with foods of every kind, why he bothers with his vegetables and fruit. In all the years I've known him it was the only time I've ever seen him look at me with disappointment. He took a long slug of wine. "There are lots of women out there," he said, "And lots of kids. Why bother having your own?"

~

A Tuscan proverb says, "All beginnings are hard." So how can you find the mental fortitude to be the first in your neighborhood to lay waste to your lawn and plant a vegetable garden? Well, the Obamas could do it . . . .Anyway, here are five good reasons why: health, wealth, flavor, environment, and to help bond your family.

Health

The health benefits of growing much of your own food are so many and so intertwining—beyond all the exercise you'll get digging and hoeing—that they could fill a book, but then you'd just keep on reading and never get out there to dynamite the lawn.

But before we start drooling about all the good things you can grow and eat using the Tuscan model, let us start with what you *will not* be eating.

In North America alone 500 million pounds of pesticides and herbicides are used every year. Even if you subtract the million pounds poured onto our lawns, that still leaves 499 million in our cheeseburgers and fries. Having your own food garden will cut profoundly into your venom diet. You may think I'm being melodramatic in using the word venom, but the suffix "-cide" is defined in my Oxford dictionary as "a substance that kills." Pesticides and herbicides are created for one reason only: to destroy living cells with as much fatality as possible. Of course, we are told that many of these venoms expire after a week or two, besides which there are laws and controls to avoid disasters. Are these the same laws and controls that so successfully governed Wall Street, the banks, and the sub-prime economy? And just how many hundred Bernie Madoffs are there in our food chain? How many in the tomato business? Or the feed lot business? Or the fast food business? Just asking.

To give us an idea of just how we got here, allow me to indulge for a moment in a quick history, mostly a downward spiral of the American farm. Until the 1940s, most farms were family farms resembling the classic one of the Davises and the Paoluccis: usually a blend of livestock, poultry, and various crops. Most farmers produced forage and feed grains for their animals using ancient, natural—and, yes, organic—systems of rotating crops and returning animal manure to fertilize the soil. Pests, too, were kept under control by having a great variety of crops in smaller fields. Along with constant crop rotation, this not only avoided the creation of veritable paradises for single pests, but also made a highly diverse environment to facilitate the habitation of pests' natural enemies. There was also a variety of cultural and biological means involving everything from placing birdhouses in orchards to attract birds that fed on pests, to physically bringing in natural enemies like the cute but voracious ladybugs to devour aphids, to Albert Koebele's Australian vedelia beetles, which, in 1888, saved the California citrus industry from destruction. The labor-intensive hoe and plow were the weed control method of the day.

Then came agribusiness.

Over 8 million people left farms in a few decades—

replaced by giant, absent corporations where profit and efficiency overrode the common sense of farming methods that worked so well for millennia. Mixed farming was replaced by thousands of acres of a single crop, creating a haven for single pests—so in came pesticides. Free-range animals were hemmed sardine-like into feedlots, where tens of thousands of them stink and ferment cheek-to-cheek, subject to disease—so in came preemptive antibiotics. The hoe and plow weren't cost effective—so in came herbicides. And they, with the help of often-devastating federal programs, have literally poisoned the land, replacing the careful family farmer with chemicals that are poisoning us all.

That is how all the venoms came to be.

Rachel Carson commented wisely on our madness: "Future historians may well be amazed at our distorted sense of proportion. How could intelligent beings seek to control a few unwanted species by a method that contaminated the entire environment and brought the threat of disease and death even to their own kind?"

Wealth

No self-respecting Tuscan would admit that he grows food with economics in mind, yet savings are enormous—much of it indirectly. When the things you grow are so flavorful— because with organic fertilizers and little water, fragrances and flavors are highly concentrated—you will suddenly increase manyfold the number of fruits and vegetables you consume, abandoning much pricier, often processed, store-bought foods.

I never loved fruits and vegetables, preferring industrially fabricated snacks, until we moved to Paris and began shopping at the open-air market that stretched for blocks under old elms. But my love for them turned into a mania in Tuscany, when Candace began to feed us from her garden. Once I ate her high-class fruits and vegetables—as opposed to the supermarket kind that tend to taste somewhat like a napkin—they leapt from 10 percent of my diet to over 60 percent in a short time. When you include the olive oil, of which we consume a pint a day with either raw vegetables or fresh Tuscan bread and over everything from meats to potatoes—and of course add in wine, my favorite fruit juice—our fruit and vegetable intake can easily touch 90 percent. It is thus easy to see how savings go far beyond what one would tend to think.

And how much can we save as a society by planting a real Tuscan food garden? Well, for a start, North Americans spend over $60 billion a year just on diets and liposuction. How much more can be saved in medical bills for curing all the ailments caused by obesity—a condition most difficult to achieve on celery sticks and apples—everything from heart disease, strokes, and diabetes, to the various cancers, caused by the venoms the store-bought goods can contain, God only knows.

~

In Florida, where pine forests and orange groves have been

cut down to make room for houses, many of the dream developments now lie unfinished. I read in the Times about Lehigh Acres where, amid abandoned houses, 220 families were waiting for free food at Faith Lutheran Church. Nearby, "Laid off construction workers in flannel shirts scavenged through trash bags at a home foreclosure, grabbing wires, CDs, anything that could be sold."

I telephoned Joseph Whalen, the president of Lehigh's Chamber of Commerce. He is a gently-spoken man understandably defensive about his town, where house prices have fallen 80% from their peak and one in four residents is on food stamps. We chatted about the future, the problems, the hopes. At the end I asked a question I had been hesitant to ask: "With all that good soil and water you have—I understand all was farmland until a few years ago—of the thousands of homes in Lehigh Acres, how many would you guess have planted orchards and vegetable gardens?"

He thought about it a while, then replied, "We don't need those things. We can get food from nearby farms."

Not to mention the bread line at Faith Lutheran Church.

Flavor

A good walk from our house, past one of the vegetable gardens, through the orchard, and beyond the pond, begin the woods. Here, in a clearing with three twisted olives, we poured a concrete slab and built a chicken coop the size of

Thoreau's cabin at Walden Pond.

We have a wonderful material to build with in Tuscany called *tufo*, sandstone—like the brownstones of Manhattan—cut into blocks and easy to stack and cement into a wall, it is unnecessary to finish inside or out. We bought twenty chicks and chickens, a half dozen ducks, five Guinea hens, two young turkeys, and some pigeons to swoop around the gardens.

It's refreshing every morning to open the gate and watch them run and waddle with great enthusiasm out into the woods. There they eat mushrooms, seeds, herbs, and berries. They wander into the orchard to peck fallen fruit, and down into the vineyards to eat the grapes we've green-pruned, and onto the compost heap to load up on kitchen scraps.

"Why?" you ask yourself, "is he boring us with these details?"

Well, unless you realize what a wonderfully varied and all-natural diet these free-range cacklers have, you will have no idea of just what amazing flavors you'll experience when you eat them roasted, basted with olive oil, with a bit of rosemary and sage stuffed under their skin. I tell you, no chicken or duck or their egg has ever tasted so good. How good the roaming turkeys tasted I won't mention because you'll die of jealousy.

And chickens, ducks, and pigeons liven up the place with their colors and their sounds—except for the goddamn rooster, who wakes me up from my sweetest sleep at 5:00

a.m. in summer, but who'll make up for this shortcoming in the oven stuffed with plums and served with roast potatoes and braised fennel.

The fruits and vegetables we grow are just as exquisite in flavors. While they don't roam around the woods and vineyards for exotic nourishment, their concentrated flavors make every one of them unforgettable: the arugula is so peppery it brings tears, the small, distorted carrots are as sweet as candy, the green peppers are both sweet and tart, and our apples and apricots, while tiny and ugly, taste so good and so juicy that when you eat, you close your eyes.

~

If we are not exposed to the inimitable flavors our home garden can yield, then how will we ever know them? How could we learn to crave them? And if we don't know the thrill and joy nature can bring, how will we learn to love her? That is why we should work tooth and nail to grow our own tomatoes, full of fragrance and full of sun.

Environment

When you grow much of your own food, saving the planet comes as a freebie. Not only do you forego herbicides, pesticides, and chemical fertilizers, which harm not just you but wildlife and groundwater, but you'll use mostly hand tools instead of the enormous, polluting machinery of commercial farming.

Then, of course, there is the great God of modern times: transportation. The average food in North America travels a staggering 1,100 miles. In our Tuscan hamlet, we average 50 steps. A Worldwatch Institute report speaks wistfully of a sustainable world of the future, warning of devastated economies and unlivable environments if we continue with mass-produced, mass-transported food. In a sustainable world, where carbon emissions must be cut by two-thirds, we "cannot be trucking vast quantities of food thousands of miles."

But the quantities of pollution saved by eliminating transport pale in comparison to the pollution caused by the processing, packaging, and marketing of our food. To be specific: the farmer receives on average only 25 cents of a dollar you spend on food. The other 75 cents go to . . . exactly.

Eating only food you grow would limit you to eating what's in season. But is that so bad? Do we have to eat strawberries in November or watermelons in January? Can we not wait with that same wonderful expectation with which we await Thanksgiving and Christmas? Do we have to have everything all the time? How dull. As Goethe said, "Nothing is harder to bear than a succession of fair days."

To Help Bond Your Family

Buster learned to hoe when he was four and the hoe was still a good foot taller than he was. Candace's vegetable garden was conquering more and more of our of land, breaking out of its original shape and weaving among rosemary bushes down into the shade of the cypress avenue. She and Buster became inseparable in the digging, hoeing, planting, and harvesting, and above all in the endless chattering that they both learned so well form the Paoluccis. Buster is obsessive; once he gets going, he can out-till the rototiller, and his dedication to perfect rows is a joy to see. As soon as he returned from the *asilo* of the nuns, the two of them would be out in the orchard or olive grove or garden working like slaves but, most vitally, being friends.

Friendships become deeper when you work together. There is something special when you need to blend your movements, to accommodate each other. And there is the pride of shared accomplishment and solace of shared failures. And is there a better place to be together with your children than on your own small plot of land, in the sunshine and fresh air, working with body, brain, and soul to provide with your own hands food for your own table? I have never seen Buster more proud or Candace more happy than when the two of them return from the garden with a basket full of things they have grown in the bare ground on their own.

And their sharing didn't stop at the door. Buster began to help Mom in the kitchen. At first he had to stand on a chair to reach the sink, and he had but menial tasks like scrubbing dirt from carrots and picking ladybugs out of lettuce, but soon he graduated to peeling and slicing until he twirled knives with the speed of a sushi chef. And later their togetherness overlapped to cooking, and even baking, all in a cloud of uninterrupted chatter.

With the years their habit of working together spread to the wine cellar, until they became a formidable team in working the winery, from fermentation to aging to tasting and entertaining journalist and wine aficionados.

And even now, when he comes home from university from thousands of miles away, some of his favorite times are spent with Candace working in the garden, the winery, or the kitchen. He and I have always done heavy work together, loading olives and hauling them down to the *frantoio* to have them milled into oil, or loading baskets of grapes and then punching down the wine, or clearing undergrowth, or chopping wood, or building paths, and we have spent days hiking and climbing mountains, on long bike outings, and playing ball; yet those earliest years he spent with mom in the kitchen and garden have formed a bond, not of mother and son, but of the best of friends; confidants. And no matter how far he might be from home, or what time of day or night, when a problem arises with school or of the soul, when he falls in love with a new woman or has just suffered a broken heart, Mom is first to hear and to be asked for advice.

And during the Christmas baking and cooking of Christmas dinner, anyone who values his life would be well advised to stay out of the *their* kitchen of swirling words and knives.

~

In Tuscany, this is how the love of food seems to be passed down, not just on a plate at dinner but in its entirety, literally from the ground up. No child I know is "taught" to plant, or dig, or harvest. No neighbor I know assigns chores to his children—Tuscan kids are much too spoiled for that—yet all the kids are out there working from a young age in every season: it's their play, it comes naturally, they find their own way to fit in. And along the way they find for themselves the best way to contribute to the family, filling its needs.

And I can honestly tell you that I have felt no greater reward as a father than to struggle away with Buster for hours at some task, no matter how back-breaking, no matter how banal, and to laugh together and curse together and get roaring pissed-off together when something goes awry, and at the end have him say, "Dad, I love working with you."

~

The love of working with your hands and the love of the land is deepest and strongest when begun at an early age. Candace spent most of her youth outside in the garden and woods, and even in Budapest my grandfather and I worked a tiny vegetable garden in the corner of a friend's yard in the Buda hills. And once we escaped from Hungary the passion took full bloom.

When we landed in Canada we had but our clothes and a hundred or so dollars my parents saved from working the winter and spring in Vienna. We lived near Vancouver in a three-room attic with a view of the mountains and a mandarin orange crate hung out the window for a fridge. But we immediately found a treasure in my stepfather's great uncle, Feribacsi. Feribacsi had a place nearby that even in retrospect seems like paradise to me. Not long before we got there, his valley had been small farms, and across the road a chicken farm still lingered, where you could take your battered egg carton and come back with it full of eggs, some still warm, some still with bits of straw sticking to the shell. Feribacsi lived with his wife, Ildiko, in a small, one-bedroom house, perfectly kept and surrounded by flowers, but it was the two acres of land around the house I really loved. There was a small lawn, an orchard, a vegetable garden, an overgrown field, and, in the back woods a great, bramble-covered abandoned chicken coop. Many years before there must have been a clearing behind the coop, because there were no trees there, only waves of brambles that washed over the roof and poured in through the windows. One spring evening, Feribacsi announced that if we wanted to have our own vegetable garden, the bramble jungle behind the chicken coop was ours.

We started hacking Sunday morning, my stepfather in the lead wielding a machete, my mother right behind tugging brambles with a rake, and me bringing up the rear with an army shovel, whacking away at berry roots that went all the way to China. Every evening after work, out we went behind the chicken coop, picked up our weapons, and attacked. It was late May. The northern evenings were long. There was still light in the sky as we walked home to our attic every night, tired as dogs but in stitches at my attempts at yodeling like Gene Autry. We slept well. We survived two weeks of hacking, sweating, and yodeling to clear that patch of dirt. Then we turned the soil. My God what soil it was. I was only eleven and knew nothing about humus or fertility, but there was something about that thick, black forest loam, the way it crumbled in your hand, the way its fragrance filled the air.

We laid out the plant beds straight and even, each as wide as the pick handle was long, then we stomped down the paths to keep the weeds from growing, and then, on the tenth of June, three months to the day after we set foot in the New World, we seeded the black soil of our almost-own piece of land.

For a week, nothing grew. We watered the barren soil each night, then walked home. I never said a word, but I had great doubts that anything would ever emerge from that empty dirt. Then one Saturday it happened. It was hot. The sun was high, the sky clear, and by late afternoon the cedar trees around us breathed a fragrance I had never smelled before. I was near the garage helping Feribacsi wash his maroon 1954 Ford, preparing it for the Sunday drive, when a joyous cry from the chicken coop cut the air. We ran. My stepdad and my mom were leaning over the seeded beds, calling "Look, look!" I thought the empty soil had finally driven them mad, but I looked anyway. I squatted by the beds and tilted my head sideways and saw, in the barren earth, lit by the sinking sun, standing in rows like miniature solders, delicate green shoots reaching toward the sky.

It was a good summer. Dennis Mitchell and I made a fort in a hollowed stump, and in the evenings we watered and weeded our garden that by August was as lush as Tarzan's jungle with radishes and parsley and celery and onions; on Sundays, we went fishing in that shallow muddy creek, and to the relief of the whole family, I completely and forever lost my urge to yodel.

And throughout that fall we were back behind the chicken coop, loading up on fresh corn, and green and yellow peppers, some of them so spicy they brought tears to your eyes, and parsnip and carrots and two sacks of potatoes, or just sitting on the coop's steps, still warm from the sun. And even on October evenings, when cold northern winter reared its frosty head, that garden kept us together not behind the coop but in the kitchen of the attic. We canned.

That piece of earth had provided food to last us through the winter. We spent the evenings gutting peppers, shredding cabbage to be pickled, slicing beats to be boiled, and peeling little onions and stuffing them in Mason jars. We built shelves in the low part of the attic, where it was coolest, to house the rows of jars full of more colors and flavors than you can name. And through the winter months the garden remained with us. It was there at every dinner each time a jar was opened with a pop, each time we crunched a pickle. It was there as clear as a summer's day with, "Remember that damned shovel," or "that huge melon" or "that slug." It was there through the muddy spring on the cleaned-off kitchen table with the colored bags of seeds and carefully penciled plans of the beds, with so much designated for this, so much for that.

Vegetable gardens held the family together for years, behind the coop, then behind our tiny house, then later behind the big house we built high on a hill. But with each place, with each year it grew a little smaller, and with each place, with each year we grew slowly apart. The only meals we shared those last years were on holidays, and there was just a row of parsley left the year my mother died.

Whether abandonment of the garden was a cause of the rift between us, or a symptom, who can say. But in those gardens there were special moments: a lot of good ones and probably more bad than I remember, but whatever else those gardens gave us, they gave us common ground. My mother had her own job and my stepfather had his, and I had school and sports and friends, and we all had all our own problems, needs, sleepless nights, and fears, but in that garden we shared and shared alike, loved it and hated it, weeded, worried, and harvested all together. Perhaps that's not much, but in a world as chaotic as ours, where ties between us loosened long ago, isolating parents, estranging children, and giving us so little common ground to share, then, at least looking back, that garden seems an island remote from senseless struggles, where not only could we shut the world out, but we could shut ourselves in alone—together.

12 ~ THE TUSCAN HOUSE

*T*he most striking things about a Tuscan house are its simplicity and solidity. In its most generic, it is like the first house you ever drew: a pitched roof, a door, and some windows. One's first reaction is, "It's so simple I could build the thing myself."

And you could.

You pick up a stone, set it down, slap in some mortar.

Our house was built by friars, and looks it. The walls bear no trace of a mason who, with trained eye, skill, and pride, selected or cut each stone to fit tight like the Etruscan wall behind our house (where you couldn't fit a cigarette paper between the stones). The walls are made of field stones, misfit, round, and most noteworthy, small; a friar's forte was not lifting and breaking rock.

Some walls are three feet thick; a few have been there over a thousand years. The house has been added onto thirteen different times, so it now wraps around the courtyard and guard tower. There are arches of many curvatures, as the Tuscans say, "*sesti*," some flat, some perfect segments of a circle, others a bit undecided as if the builder began with a clear idea in the morning but ended up more daring after the wine of lunch.

Since no one bothered much with squares, levels, or even plumb lines, the walls often tilt, or bulge, or undulate as if alive. Yet what is ever-present is the strength, the permanence. The roofs are held up by great oak or chestnut beams, whole trunks just stripped of bark and set with the curve up in place, and above them on smaller runners are terracotta tiles that are almost as long-lasting as the stones. Even the gutters and downspouts are of copper that lasts for generations.

The Tuscan house, much like everything around it, makes sense in every detail. The rooms are small; there are no frills, no extras, because creating them and maintaining them would take time away from more important things. While the floors of the wealthy in Florence and Siena are often of marble, the country Tuscans discovered something cheaper and simpler to work, but almost as long-lasting: the terracotta tile. Under old shoes with tacks they lasted centuries; under modern sneakers they should last millennia.

Even the most modest houses have kitchen counters of marble because nothing can damage them. The sinks, too, are of stone and if they wear round a corner or erode a hollow, that just adds to their beauty.

The outside walls and roofs require no maintenance.

The great wood doors and wooden windows need a pass of stain every few years, but apart from that a home is to enjoy and not constantly maintain or repair.

~

Unawares, Tuscan houses were light years ahead environmentally: common sense enforced energy savings. The stone walls are excellent for extending the seasons, storing summer heat well into the fall and the cool of spring into the hot days of June. The small windows help, too, doubly so with an ingenious insulating system: instead of curtains there are tightly-closing wooden shutters on the inside. Not only do they create a dead airspace, but, being wood, they out-insulate any layer of glass. And they also bless you with absolute darkness, so you can sleep in on the weekends well past sunrise.

Against the summer heat, many houses are fit with *persiane*, louvered shutters which keep out the sun but allow air circulation to avoid heat buildup, or *sportelli*, solid wooden ones. July and August in Tuscany can be scorching hot, but by closing the shutters and louvers every morning and opening windows wide at night to let in the cool air—not to mention the frog concert—the house remains comfortable without the cost, noise, or enormous energy consumption of air conditioning.

~

To give an idea of the simplicity of the layout, the best house to describe is the Paoluccis'. A single, long hallway divides the house in two. To the right opens the *cucina*, the kitchen; beyond it a door leads to a cellar where the olive oil, sausages, *prosciutti*, preserves, and root plants are kept in the dark, freshened by an earth floor.

To the left are three bedrooms and then a bathroom at the end. The whole thing is no more than fifteen hundred square feet.

The kitchen is, and always has been, the center of Tuscan life. At the Paoluccis' an enormous fireplace covers one wall. Its great brick hood is supported by stone columns with huge lintel in between, and below the hood on a raised hearth—inside the fireplace, really—are two low benches where you sit on winter nights. In a corner of the kitchen is an ancient marble sink, next to it a wood stove for heat and roasting meats and a gas stove, and beside that a tiny fridge; there is no use for a big one, for Tuscans eat whatever they can fresh. In a far corner is a couch and in the middle two tables, one with a marble top ideal for kneading and rolling dough, the other covered with oilcloth where the family eats. For the big Sunday lunch with company the tables are joined as one.

The kitchen is where the family lives. This is where, before the girls were married, Eleonora did her homework, where Carla, her older sister, ironed and sewed and argued with her boyfriend, where their mother, Rosanna still cooks and fills jars with stewed tomatoes or plum jam, where Nonna, the grandmother, grills mushrooms by the fire or dries them, sliced fine, to be put away and served with *tagli-*

atelle on bleak winter nights. And this is where—with hands gnarled by a life of work—she knits mittens and hats and wool socks for the family, and this is where Paolucci sits by the fire or helps his wife, plays with his grandchildren and welcomes his neighbors.

And this is where twice a day the family sits down to an enormous meal of pasta, meat, salad, cheese, fruit, and wine.

So that's the Paoluccis' kitchen, where they spend most of their lives. If they were to build themselves a yawning dining room, a spacious living room, and a den for the TV, as far as I can tell, they would gain nothing at all. But they might just lose that most precious thing: each other's company. They might lose someone to yell at, or touch, or to make them smile out of the blue. They might stop being as natural and easygoing as you can only be around those you trust. They might forget how to be tolerant of each other. They might, unintentionally, imperceptibly, and perhaps irreversibly, grow apart. They might, little by little, forget how to be a family.

Where Have All Our Houses Gone?

What's remarkable about Tuscans is not just what they have, but all the things they have chosen to live without. It's as if they learned long ago the true meaning of "there is no such thing as a free lunch." They seem to know that for each acquisition, whether as simple as a garage or as thrilling as a new kitchen, you are giving not just money, but what it took to earn it: a portion of your life.

~

Not long ago, we too lived in reasonable houses, where our eat-in kitchen was the heart of the house, with its warm stove, big table, and a hundred magic smells, the many hours of the family together, making meals, eating, cleaning up, talking—about nothing, about everything. But lately, perhaps because of our newly found affluence—or, more correctly, the new-found ease with which we can accumulate more debt—our houses have become sad enormities where couples or small families rattle about like stones in an empty barrel.

I was stunned by an article in the Times about a couple in Florida who bought—in February of 2009 in the depth of the recession—a *weekend* condominium of 4,000 square feet. After we spend the frantic week apart, are not the weekends for being with those we love? To renew our closeness? Our intimacies? How can you be intimate in a coliseum? Or was the place bought for show? To impress who?

NPR did a story on the ever-expanding American Dream House. It seems it's growing faster than our waistlines. In 1950, the average square footage of a new single-family home was 980 square feet, but by 2004 it had more than doubled to 2,400, even while families got ever smaller. Margot Adler, who centered the broadcast on an 11,000-square-foot home, wondered, "Is it wealth? Is it greed? Or are there more subtle things going on?"

One Hamptons' architect thought it was self-defense. "Who knows when the next 9/11 will happen?" she said. "These houses represent safety—the bigger the house, the bigger the fortress."

Fortress? Was she kidding? I attempted to build our chicken coop following the construction methods used for most Hamptons houses—stud walls, sheetrock, plastic siding, roof-tiles made of tar—but Giancarlo, who has been helping in our winery since we started, refused to lift a hammer. "The wood will rot, the roof will leak, and if the rooster gets angry he'll kick the whole thing down."

We ended up building it out of blocks of sandstone. Like a real fortress near us built in 1422.

⁓

For John Stilgoe, a history professor at Harvard, "The big house represents the atomizing of the American family. Each person not only has his or her television—each person has his or her bathroom. Some of these houses are literally designed with three playrooms for two children. This way, the family members rarely have to interact. And the notion of compromise is simply out."

Our enormous houses, like our enormous cars, are symptoms of a culture that has abandoned common sense, lost the ability to reason.

We once went with friends for Christmas cocktails to a house in Scottsdale, Arizona: serious money, vast lawn, a columned portico the size of the Parthenon, and a cathedral entrance as voluminous as Brunelleschi's dome in Florence. Off in the distance was the curving staircase from *Gone with the Wind,* and on it, the entire Phoenix Boy's Choir, Christmas—caroling their pre-pubescent hearts out. When they left, out came card tables, dice tables, and a half-dozen roulette wheels complete with croupiers, and onward went the night, celebrating the humble birth of Christ.

The rest of the house, all 12,000 square feet of it, was equally homey. There was the Jungle room, with stuffed and mounted wildlife; the Alpine room, with doilies, carved chairs, and a cuckoo clock; the Pirate room, from which I recoiled too fast to take note; and, of course, the Wild West room, with guns and tomahawks and a life-sized wooden Indian. Schizophrenia unchained. And the hosts, with embarrassed eyes and cemented smiles, talked about their life and how they felt the time had come to make a "statement." The only true statement came when the clock struck twelve and the bird screamed out, "Cuckoo!!"

~

When Candace and I first moved in together, it was into a Volkswagen van that totaled 28 square feet—including the driver's seat. We spent four months in that van vagabonding through Mexico, Guatemala, El Salvador (before the war), Nicaragua (ditto), Costa Rica, Belize, and Panama. We lived on five dollars a day and that included gas.

Nine years later, in West Vancouver, we built a house on the beach at the bottom of a cliff. It was four stories high;

you came in via a footbridge to the top floor from the driveway. It was all glass, front and back, with the ocean ahead and the verdant cliff behind; the rest was clad inside and out in cedar. It was an architectural wonder exactly *one hundred times bigger* than the van. And felt as cozy as the Astrodome. After a year of shouting to each other from one empty room to the next, we moved into a tiny Parisian flat, where we felt comfortingly near each other, where we felt at home.

And looking back now—even from the luxury of a stone house in Tuscany—those four months in that van were the best months of our lives.

~

It's not just the modest size of Tuscan houses that impresses—Marco, our electrician, who has six employees, just finished his house of 800 square feet, which in view, coziness, and quality is a pleasure to behold—but it's all the things the houses *don't* have that leave such an impression.

No matter how stunning the house, however rich its owner, I cannot think of a house or a villa in Tuscany that has, leading to it, a driveway that is paved. Don't roll your eyes—it's a good place to start. Look at your own driveway: one thousand square feet of glittering black tar. Have you the faintest notion of what you paid for that? Perhaps it's not a fortune, you can pay it off in a month, but isn't that the point? A month? A whole month so the car can roll on tar instead of stone?

Of course, we seldom evaluate our consumption by

what Thoreau called "the true cost of a thing." We take life the way it comes, too often in a choice-less package. And we sign on the dotted line without ever thinking that the fine print we failed to read might have entrapped us for life.

Then there's the garage most Tuscans do without. In North America it's a veritable palace. Windows, bright lights, electric doors, heat, Muzak—a Chinese village of thirty could live there in great comfort. And over the years, with interest and insurance, a new roof here, a new door there, you'll come close to blowing another hundred Gs; after taxes, the wages of two years. Now, can you imagine that if you had the choice of fishing by a creek, sitting by the ocean, or sailing the South Pacific, you'd choose instead to rise two years' of mornings, shave-shower-slurp-gobble-run, drive in hellish traffic road-raging to the stable, get in the harness, spend eight hours tugging, jerking, slipping in the stinking streets, worrying, ass-kissing, taking the bloody whip, looking over your shoulder for the day to end? Can you imagine doing that for two years of your life, so that pile of soon-to-be-scrap metal can stay out of the rain?

If you can, close the book; I'm talking to the wrong guy.

The Living Room

Is there a more misnamed room in our culture than this one? Can we call slouching on a couch watching dots flicker on a screen "living"? If that's life, exactly what's a coma?

How many days a year is this empty space filled with

the passionate conversation or bubbling laughter of friends and neighbors who drifted in and sat down for a beer, a glass of wine, or a cup of tea and discussed the ills of the world, their lives, or their zucchinis? And when was the last time a mob of uncles, nephews, cousins, aunts, and grannies draped themselves over the furniture with the ease and soft boredom of family? Are these not the things we can honestly call "living"? If our living rooms are just for the tube, wouldn't we have been better off planting a little grove in its place so we could look at some birds and trees, some real reality? Just think how much smaller the mortgage would have been, and how much more peaceful our sleep every night.

The Dining Room

If all goes well, we might sit down once a day in this bare room to have a meal. And too often it's take-out, or something heated from a box. Do we need a whole room for that? Is a table in the kitchen not good enough?

The Mechanized Kitchen

One of modern life's prides seems to be a vast kitchen full of islands and peninsulas and enough appliances to founder the Titanic. It's as if it was the gear that cooked the food and not us. Rosanna and Nonna and Candace use nothing but a simple stove or the fireplace and cook up miracles, with their only mechanical aids a ladle and a corkscrew.

As Mark "the minimalist" Bittman wrote, "When it comes to kitchens, size and equipment don't count nearly as much as devotion, passion, and common sense. To pretend otherwise—to spend tens of thousands of dollars or more on a kitchen . . . is to fall into the same kind of silly consumerism that leads people to believe that the right bed will improve their sex life."

The superstar chef Mario Batali concurs. "Only bad cooks blame the equipment. I can make almost every dish in my restaurants on four crummy electric burners with a regular oven."

Much of our must-have gear defies common sense. Take the garbage disposal. What does it do beside make noise and whip compostable food into unreachable places? Or the garbage compressor. It costs a lot, takes up space, and gives you hernias carrying garbage out. I mean, what's the big thrill in having compressed garbage?

Then there's the dishwasher. We had one once and I could never figure out why, if we had a machine that washed dishes, *I* had to wash each dish first by hand. I mean, wine glasses were always hand jobs, pots and pans ditto, and the rest I had to rinse or wipe and then load in the machine. Then I had to unload it and often wipe it dry. Now that's not exactly sitting back eating bonbons. And the very thing you need is always dirty anyway, buried in the washer so you have to dig it out and chisel off the now hard-crusted goo. Is that saving time?

And the electric can opener. Was the old one too taxing because you had to use two hands? Or were the ten seconds of manual labor too demeaning?

Forget the hundred other gadgets: electric knives, choppers, grinders, pulpers and slashers, most of which sit long-forgotten in some hard-to-get-at cupboard. Let us just grant that the modern kitchen is a joy to the eye . . . but where are those unforgettable home-cooked meals? And, just as importantly, where are the people?

The Laundry Room

Excuse me for prying, but why do dirty socks and undies need a room of their own? Some claim it's so you can iron there, but ironing boards are portable; you can iron anywhere, and who wants to iron shut away with a machine? Isn't ironing more fun where there are people?

Then there's the dryer.

Not long ago our back yards were alive with clean laundry dancing in the breeze. And hanging out the laundry was not only a bit of exercise but also a social act, a time for a backyard chat with neighbors. It also worked in the city—the narrow streets of Naples and Venice still fly their colored banners on laundry day. So why are our clotheslines gone? And not only forgotten but in some places *forbidden*. Is this for real? We can park a Humvee—the most vulgar insult to human intelligence—in public, but freshly washed clothes on a line we find offensive?

A friend in Tuscany, educated and well traveled,

laughed when I told him about a machine that dries clothes. He thought I was kidding. Why, he asked, would a sane person pay for a machine—that in some estimates uses up 10 percent of our continent's electricity—instead of using the sun and wind? I told him that in North America you didn't dry your clothes on a line because your neighbor might think you poor. Sadly enough, that he understood.

And sure, a dryer may save us a few minutes, but the question is, for what? To spend more time staring at the tube? Or to surf the net to find some new gadget to buy, or to hear which airhead said what inanity to whom? Is that really preferable to standing in the back yard, getting a little air?

I fear the truth is that we live by rote; we become addicted to whatever is shoved before us. Perhaps Darwin is wrong; we're not descendants of apes but of sheep, whose only noteworthy trait is that they love to follow.

13 ~ BUILD YOUR OWN LIFE

The best description of Tuscans—besides spontaneous—may well be independent. While this quality most often results in novel experiences of the most enjoyable kind, it does at times leave you pleading for smelling salts.

We had owned our new Volkswagen but a few months when one day I decided to check the level of the oil. While reaching down, my credit card slipped from my shirt pocket and vanished into the tightly-packed motor compartment. Mancini, the gas station owner, disappeared for a second but returned armed with a screwdriver and crescent wrench. Well. Compared to him, Attila the Hun was as delicate as a midwife. The wrench flashed and the screwdriver turned and within minutes half the motor was lying in pieces on the ground. Scattered randomly. Regaining my breath after a mild stroke, I began sorting the pieces so they could be remounted in the reverse order, but Mancini would have none of it; he reached here, grabbed there and slam-bam-thank-you-ma'am, he tightened the last screw and shut the hood. I was speechless; not because of his speed, but because three pieces were still lying in my hands. I held them out to him making gasping sounds, but he just put his arm on my shoulder and said comfortingly, "Germans. They make things much too complicated."

The Volkswagen ran fine. In fact, better than before.

Then there was Bindi, the plumber.

We had a new furnace installed to heat our water, which in turn heated the house. It was a magnificent, compact Swedish masterpiece, a Turbo something. Bindi installed it, checked it, double-checked it, then dragged me outside to point out that not a trace of smoke escaped, only water vapor. Then he sniffed the air and turned glum. He went in, shut off the furnace, and in seconds dismantled it, bringing to light a jewel of a casting with a hundred tiny holes through which the turbo blew air. Then he whipped out a miniscule round file and began to enlarge each and every hole. While I, panic-stricken, ranted about voided warranties and broken environmental laws, he silently finished filing the holes, put it all back together, and ate a banana. Then he went outside, sniffed the air, and, without the slightest change of expression, held out his hands like some trapeze artists who had performed a deadly triple twist.

"And what if it blows up and kills us?" I complained angrily.

He pondered for a moment, folded his banana peel, and said, "We'll cross that bridge when we come to it."

A week later, after having one glass of wine too many at Inaldo's, the local junkman-cum-antique dealer's, I calmly backed our car over the concrete edge of a deep stairwell. It hung ceremoniously in midair, close to Bindi playing cards at the bar's outside table.

He walked over calmly and stared.

"It'll take two tow trucks," I grumbled. "To lift up front and back so we don't damage anything."

"Maybe," Bindi said.

"I'll go get them. Do you think it might tip over before I come back?"

"Maybe."

I ran. When I came back in Mancini's tow truck, the Matra was surrounded by people and I heard Bindi's voice, *"Uno, due, tre!"*

There was shouting, then everyone returned to the game of cards, leaving the Matra they had lifted with bare hands back on solid ground. Bindi, shuffling the deck, beamed with self-contentment. "Where there's a will," but Mancini broke in, "There's a stubborn mule."

~

Tuscans are fearless; they'll try anything.

I have seen Paolucci attempt seemingly impossible maneuvers on steep hills with his tractor; I have seen Lamberto without having ever lifted a mason's trowel build a perfectly fitted hundred-foot-long stone wall. Pasquino, a truck driver by trade, has no fear of butchering and dressing his and the neighbors' pigs, and our chief stonemason, Fosco, who lead the restoration of our house, didn't hesitate to tell me that parts of my design stank and that the covered out-door dining area I drew up should be moved 20 feet to the south, and be on four stone columns on its own, because it would feel much more dramatic free-standing than attached. It turned out to be the best part of the house.

~

All of the above may seem like trifling details, but they reflect a self-assurance that manifests itself in every phase of Tuscan life. Perhaps for this reason, more than any other, most Tuscans work for themselves *and* ply their trade with pride. And perhaps this is why they are undisturbed by the prospects of recessions or depressions, because they feel sure that they can just invent something new and land on their feet again. This is no small thing. As I mentioned, Tuscans grow up doing work for fun. This makes trusting their own hands and their own judgments second nature, which in turn makes anything possible—and they know that making it pos-sible is entirely up to them.

~

I have often been asked how Candace and I had the courage to tackle things like restoring a stone ruin, planting a vine-yard, and challenging our world-famous neighbors in wine-making.

I answer that watching Paolucci, Bindi, and other

neighbors improvise everything but brain surgery gave me confidence to tackle anything at all. I must admit that being brought up in Hungary, with its post-war ghost-economy where everyone had to do something inventive on the side to survive, makes trying something you know nothing about seem the very essence of a successful life.

This ability to reinvent oneself, to sail confidently into unknown waters, seems to be even more needed today, with our ever-deeper recessions in which many jobs are simply and permanently eliminated. The urgency is made more dire by the fact that we have been trained for decades by large corporations and franchises to suppress not only our independence but also our creativity as we performed jobs that resembled more and more the mind-numbing production line.

~

One of my most memorable lessons on how to survive came when I was eleven, the week after we escaped from Hungary. The Austrians housed us in old airport barracks, where one day a very well-dressed gentleman, a Mr. Edlinger, appeared and said he was looking for experts in the textile industry to work at his factory. A young man who we had met during the night of our escape while crawling through an icy ditch instantly put up his hand. The fact that he had only ever planted trees didn't give him pause. He got the job and within a few months became one of the most respected workers at the plant. His sangfroid stayed with me. So when, seven years later, I needed a place to live while in university, undertaking building that houseboat seemed to me the most natural thing in the world.

When I mentioned to Bindi how fearlessness in tackling new challenges seems to be inherent in most Tuscans, he replied without hesitation, "If another human being can do it, why not I?"

An old friend, social psychologist Norm Cleary, confirmed this. He found that he could teach almost any job to anyone in a week. And he observed that, apart from instantly recognizable intelligence, what really mattered more than anything was self-confidence. Indeed, the speed of learning seemed to depend on whether one viewed the learning experience as a potential for success or a potential for failure. If you grow up the Tuscan way—active around the house—and whatever you try is rewarded and admired, it's most likely that you will have a natural self-confidence. Conversely, if your childhood was limited to the virtual world of TV and video games, it's understandable that complex "real world" tasks would daunt if not terrify you.

And had the activities you were rewarded for in your youth entailed physical and mental work that related to survival—like helping to build something, or grow something, or cook something on your own—then would it not naturally follow that you'd have great faith in your own brain and hands to look after yourself? And knowing you could look after yourself if need be, you would not fall into the "despair, discouragement, and depression" felt by many who lose their job and fear the future?

~

There are numerous major reasons to lead a do-it-yourself life, which can be defined as making what you want yourself—house, sailboat, cabin, fence—as opposed to getting a job to earn enough to eventually buy it.

Economy

As with the food garden, much saving comes from de-intermediation, which means eliminating the middleman. You will not be paying for other people's overhead, profit, taxes, and miscalculations. Hence every move you make is to achieve a direct and visible end.

You will also save through your ability to improvise or just to take time to search for the best deal on material, something professionals working by rote will not take the time to do, and if they do, they sure as hell won't pass the savings on to you.

When I started building that houseboat, after spending $150 for the scow, I had but six hundred dollars left from working three months of that summer. So I began to scrounge. The two-by-fours I bought from a house-wrecker, the plywood for the walls had flaws and so were discounted, the fireplace I built out of a small cement hopper, the brand new wall-to-wall sisal rug was from a lady who found it too rough on her bare feet, the insulation was scrap sheets from a Styrofoam plant, and both the stove and the little fridge had cosmetic damage about which the underside of my counter couldn't give a damn.

My total expenses were $550. Had I hired a builder to just go ahead and build it, it would have cost me ten times that amount. And I would have missed out on the best part of scrounging: every foray to wreckers, scrap metal warehouses, used marine discounters, and even lumberyards became an adventure and a chance to meet some unusual characters, most of whom were all too eager to help with suggestions and deals.

Once you've scavenged and built your own houseboat, packing up your life and moving to Tuscany is a piece of cake.

Pride

I honestly can't think of a more rewarding—or frustrating, maddening, and infuriating—undertaking than building your own house. To use an old cliché, "Every day is Christmas." There are few more ego-boosting times in life than that quiet hour at the end of each day when you get to stand back and survey what you have accomplished since morning. I remember building that big house on the beach, where we often worked at great heights from dawn to winter dusk. At the end of the day I put away the tools, swept up cuttings and chips to make the next day's work easier, then sat down in a corner with the darkening sea at my feet and stared at what we'd done. Those were special times. I don't remember that kind of pride once the house was done.

But a different pride, more subtle and more lasting, remains with you. Every part of your house will carry memories, a certain day, a laugh, a small disaster, some event that will bring back, for years, that time you built your own life.

Quality

No one will build your house with as much care as you will. There is, I think, bred into us all enough common sense that we will not build something for ourselves that might require early repair. Developers must constantly think of profit, hence they tend to go for margins rather than the best quality at the best price. Since most manufactured things manage to survive while the warranty lasts, the problems begin later, when only you will be left to shoulder the burden.

The relationship with sub-trades also insures a higher quality. When you build your own, you will get to know the craftsman in a budding friendship. This naturally results in more dedication by them, and hence higher quality, but just as important is the often unwritten guarantee—the conscience part—that such a relationship supplies. This rapport can give you peace of mind.

Rebuilding Colombaio, we used wooden doors and windows. We chose Arte 5 for the quality of their work. About two years later, one of the doors on the south side, beaten by sun and rain, warped slightly so that the closing mechanism felt stiff. Still in my North American mode, I phoned up in a panic to see if the guarantee had expired. Ugo said he'd come and have a look. He came, looked, hummed, and toiled. I figured he would adjust the hinge, so I went about my chores. When I came back, I was shocked: he had replaced the whole complex mechanism that went from the top of the door to the bottom, with four interlocking parts. I blanched and asked how much the work would cost. Ugo smiled. "A glass of wine."

"But the guarantee," I pressed. "When will it expire?"

He looked up, crossed himself, then said, "The day I die."

Knowing the knowable

The last reason to build your own is that since you put it together, you'll probably remember how to take it back apart. I certainly feel more tranquil knowing that should something break, I can fix it on my own. It's a bit like having a doctor in the house. In this age of anxiety, when almost every object is too complex to repair, knowing how to fix the basics is reassuring indeed.

This is a big thing when you live in deep country, and an even bigger thing if you want, like we did, to spend a year at sea.

Armed with cocky self-confidence after finishing the houseboat, Candace and I decided to get a sailboat and gunkhole around the Pacific. A perfect dream, with one hitch: money. Or, more correctly: No money.

We saw the elegant brochures of an all-wood interior finished like a yacht. But the price of that completed boat was $30,000, and with everything liquidated we could raise only nine. So we decided to buy the hull and deck and build the rest: all interior furniture, floors, bulkheads, hatches, companionways, everything. Talk about babes in the woods! When the hull and deck arrived in a small yard in Newport Beach, where we would spend the next year finishing it out, it looked, from a distance, like any boat in dry-dock. Then we put a ladder against the hull, climbed up, and looked below. Now close your eyes and imagine an enormous, empty bleach bottle, which, with all its compound curves and weird angles, you have to, with your own feeble hands, turn into a cruising yacht. Now *that* is horror.

But after more than a year of work we went to sea with the comforting knowledge of how everything went together.

~

Once we finished restoring Colombaio, we began to plant 15 acres of vines. We could have given out the whole thing in contract but preferred to do it on our own. Doing each step yourself, from turning the soil, to planting the vines, to planting poles and setting up wires for guides, reassures you like only knowledge can. It's difficult to explain but if I don't know every step, I feel the same unease I do in foreign lands; I feel like a visitor, almost an intruder, instead of feeling the soothing comfort of being safely at home.

14 ~ HOME-MADE FUN

*T*he view from the *piazza* in front of Mireno's bar is always worth a stare. The moon rises behind the distant town of Sant'Angelo in Colle and lights up the volcano that looms across the valley. Cypresses stand like black candles against the mist and only swooping owls disturb the solemn "Madonna *puttana,*" "Madonna, you whore," from the card players inside.

With Camigliano's population down to 19 that year, it was a quiet evening at Mireno's, the air filled with smoke, the tables filled with men, while the women sat in the *piazza* in the moonlight exchanging opinions on how best to murder husbands.

Someone, no one remembers who, decided it was time for Camigliano to get lively again. He suggested that once a year they should have a grand feast of the best traditional local dishes out in the *piazza*. The idea was that if they got 50 paying clients, they'd turn enough profit to replace the broken tiles in the playground of the abandoned school. They put posters all around Montalcino with a number for reservations and prayed someone would call. That first year, 200 hungry people lined the narrow street. The next year more than 600 came, and the year after they had to do four meals through the weekend with 800 people sitting down for *each*. Camigliano was awash in a sea of Liras.

After the first dinner, the townspeople remained in the *piazza* and sang and danced 'til dawn. Then someone thought, why not have people dance here every weekend? They built an outdoor disco. More than 500 show up from as far as Florence and Rome to dance the night away. Now they're drowning in Euros.

But it's not just about the money. All the townspeople, as well as those from the surrounding countryside, help in organizing and working, sharing in the pride. With the money they have earned, they rebuilt the old school into a community hall. And they work together and have dinners together and take weekend trips together. They have become the best of neighbors.

Other small Tuscan towns outdo Camigliano. Monticchiello has an outdoor folk theater that, for two weeks in July, performs plays the townspeople write. Montepulciano has an international festival of theater and music that lasts for the month of August, with the world's best artists performing in courtyards, palaces, and churches.

Nearby Torrita has a month-long blues festival; Pienza, San Quirico, and Montalcino a mixed festival of music, drama, and film.

And it's not just the summer that is so filled with life, most events take long months or the whole year to prepare. The togetherness and the feeling of accomplishment, can be seen on every face.

~

And there is one other thing about entertainment in small towns and the country, whether it's Tuscany or Vermont or a plateau in New Mexico. Just as you are responsible for the work in your own fields or gardens, so you have to make up or create your own fun. And just as the satisfaction gained from working for yourself, with your own hands, whether it's building a stone wall or digging up spuds or putting up jams for winter, is almost beyond compare, so will be the home-made fun you invent on your own. For just as watching any World Series pales compared to playing softball with your friends, so most store-bought entertainment fades and is forgotten; while a family afternoon spent fishing at a stream, or a moonlit walk on a frozen, fresh-snow-covered lake, will stay vivid in your memory for the rest of your days.

I'm not sure you can ask any more from life.

15 ~ THE TUSCAN
FAMILY BUSINESS

*M*onteriggioni is a unique medieval town. Its hill is symmetrical, the hilltop leveled, so the great walls that surround it hide all the houses from outside eyes, and the outside world from the eyes of those inside. Standing within its walls, in its great central *piazza*, or in its few narrow streets, or under its shading trees, you feel inviolably secure. It's true that now and then an urge to breach the walls overcomes you, to run out the single gate or climb up into a turret just to get a glimpse of the world outside, but that glimpse seems soon to suffice and you turn back gladly into the town's embracing arms.

Some years ago, a reporter from Minnesota Public Radio flew in to interview me about my new book, *A Reasonable Life*. I suggested we meet at Il Pozzo, a small, family-run restaurant on the main *piazza*. We ate and drank and started to discuss at length the secrets of Tuscany; what has made and kept it so beautiful, what works so well that it makes us all fall in love. It was a very good lunch with equally good wine, and the owner, who spoke some English from having spent some months in Brooklyn, checked discretely from time to time to make sure we were fine. We had finished our meal, and we were the last ones there, but he worked around us, always at a distance to let us talk in peace, over-hearing what we were saying and smiling now and then. At last he could control himself no longer, he came over, his eyes flashed with passion, and he blurted, much too loudly, "Please tell America that in Italy, *la famiglia regge ancora,* that the family still holds." And he clenched his fist to show the strength of his grip, as strong as his town's walls.

~

In the hills of Tuscany, the family business holds families together more strongly still. And here I'm not just talking about the family farm or vineyard, which is often passed down with jealously guarded pride, but about many crafts-men who pass their skills onto their children and end up working with them: cabinet makers, blacksmiths, stonema-sons, and of course the cooks in their own restaurants. And as of late, so do the professionals. Both pharmacists in town have their children work in their most lucrative shops, and Piccardi, the building engineer with his own consulting firm, has his architect son Alessandro and his daughter Francesca, an engineer, working with him.

The most visible family businesses are, of course, the restaurants. In our town of Montalcino, nearly all are "family".

Our North American mentality would instantly object, insisting that a family business is as medieval as Monteriggioni, where the massive walls might provide safety, but also suffocate by blocking out the world. Yet that safety—financial, emotional, and social—which the family business provides, seems to far outweigh its confining restrictions, for most kids come to it and stay with joy and pride.

Il Marrucheto is a rare *trattoria*, specializing in fish 20 miles from the sea. In North America that distance is trivial, but in Italian minds it's in the middle of the continent. It is an unpretentious locale near Castello Banfi, on the edge of the zone delineated for Brunello. Worker-priced Tuscan lunches attract regular daily patrons-for $15 you get a pasta dish, a second course of veal, pork or lamb prepared however you like, a vegetable side dish, un quarto di vino, a quarter liter of wine, a bottle of mineral water, and of course an espresso. But Il Marrucheto, run by the Del Regno family with a friendly dignity and relentless attention to freshness and detail, has become known to gourmets from Florence to Rome. It fascinates with an amazingly broad fish menu, from filleted fresh sardines bathed in capers, parsley, and olive oil, to baby octopus tied in cheesecloth and simmered slowly in a broth of tomatoes, olive oil, garlic, and black olives.

Carmine Del Regno, the father, does the cooking, and it is not his job but his passion—or, more correctly, his obsession. Although they don't open for lunch until 12, he has his kitchen fired up daily by seven, baking mouth-watering deserts from almond, pear, and *mascarpone* cakes to the tastiest, berry tarts and the best Tarte Tatin you ever had. He once cooked in a five-star restaurant on France's Moselle River, where he bought the latest catch from fishermen twice a day, and the marriage between the cuisines of Northern France and the Amalfi Coast, where he was born, has resulted in unforgettable dishes. For his favorite customers, he'll often create something special on a whim. And if you ask Carmine why he goes to all this trouble, what besides the long, tiring hours he gets out of it, he says with artless modesty, "I enjoy making people happy."

His wife Amelia looks after ordering the food, and of course gives him a hand in the kitchen; the older son Enzo, in his thirties, orders the wines, runs the bar, and serves, while his younger brother Federico runs the pizza oven and fills in here, there, and everywhere at once. We have been friends for nearly two decades—going to the Del Regnos' is like going home to Mom. This is not just a platitude, it's a feeling expressed by many of the patrons. For while it is true that the portions are generous and the flavors complex, it is the relaxed, lively atmosphere that makes most regulars, regulars. The Del Regnos run the place as if they were at home—which they are. They come and sit and eat and drink with you, gossip and bitch and moan or just bust your *palle*.

One night with the family, over some bottles of wine, we tried to pin down the pros and cons of a family business, and as far as we could tell they boil down to two cons: One, it's difficult to change jobs, for if you decide to go it's a shock to the whole family. And the second is the emotional intensity of being with those you love.

But we found a plethora of pros. First, you can rest assured that, unless you burn the building to the ground, you won't get fired. Then there is the atmosphere: you *are* always among family. And since Italian families are very close to start with, having shared most meals, much spare time, and every holiday all their lives, a general mood of relaxation pervades. As Enzo put it, "I don't really feel I'm working, I'm just at home having fun."

Knowing each other so well means it's easy to read moods, tolerate foibles, and with little effort bring out the best in the other, who, in turn, can do the same to you.

And tensions that can build up at work find ready release in Italian families, where everyone is used to spontaneous sincerity—which, in North America, we refer to as "yelling." The best, though non-Tuscan, example of this is Al Bacareto—my home away from home—near Campo Santo Stefano in Venice, where Emilio and Anna, with their sons Adriano and Fede, run what most agree is the best classic *osteria* in the city. I eat with a handful of regulars—who have had lunch there daily for going on twenty years—at the family table near the kitchen door. The congenial bustle is that of *carnevale*, or a ballet in fast-forward, or a circus when the lions have somehow fled the cage. At times family tempers fly with verbal put-downs across the room, and the regulars join in and take sides or banter until it all sounds like a Rossini opera.

This atmosphere of home creates in the family—aside from occasional hysterics—a palpable calm. Since there are no chiefs, only Indians, everyone falls naturally into the roll that suits him best, a role that can be alternated or exchanged. The place is yours; when something needs doing, you just go and do it.

Then there are the open working hours. You don't need to arrive on time and punch a clock, as long as what needs to be done gets done in time. And even if it doesn't, nobody dies. The regulars are easy: if the service is slow they can wait, or they chip in clearing tables, or getting their own water, bread, or wine—no need for apologies, they feel all the more at home for it.

Within the working day you can go at the pace you feel best with at the time, or sit down to have a rest, or go for a bit to have a short lie in the sun, or run home to your dearest for a bit of love.

During the year, you can take days or weeks off when you need to. No Tuscan restaurant is open every day; each has its day of rest agreed to with other restaurants around them so the regulars of one don't go hungry that day, but if you need more time off, the family complies. And since the main long-term aim of the family is its own happiness, making each other happy becomes as reflexive as blinking. If the "spread of happiness" test, which shows how one's happiness affects co-workers, were to be applied to family members running their own business, then, judging by my own family, who has worked together making wine for years, the needle would not only jump but jam at the extreme.

Then, of course, there's the money. The wages you receive are as flexible as the time. At Il Marrucheto there are no paydays or paychecks, there is only the till. When you need money, you take it; when you don't, you're expected to leave it for those who do. "And however little you make," Enzo laughed explaining, "you must remember the money you save by not having the dog, the one you need to kick when work goes badly that day. He waved his hand around the room, "Here, we take turns. One day you're the dog, the next day you do the kicking."

When hard times hit, as they did this year, they don't seem to hit as hard when everyone suffers and worries equally. And, sticking together, they manage to make do, get by.

As the evening wore on, the ideas wore down, until someone mentioned the word *fiertà,* or pride. Then, starting with the dad, everyone chipped in until Candace and I were dragged into the midst and agreed that in the do-it-yourself-life, having the whole family involved just amplifies it. And we all agreed that this was not just the simple pride of beholding something you have created, whether it's a plate of *gnocchi ai frutti di mare,* dumplings with seafood, or wine, but also that most rewarding look of joy on your clients' faces. For you are not only proud of what you made and served, but you are proud too of your place, proud of yourself, your life, and your whole family. And though you never put it in words, it shows on your face, and spreads like some plague of happiness from person to person, house to house, hamlet to hamlet, town to Tuscan town.

And I just had to tell them of the couple in North Carolina who ordered some of our Syrah, with which they fell in love at a friend's. They asked us to rush it because they were about to leave on a tramp steamer cruise and wanted our wine on board for the evening of their fiftieth anniversary. There was slim chance of it arriving, but it went by courier anyway. The day they were to leave, they had given up hope, packed their bags, loaded the car, and started to back up when the courier blocked their driveway. With the wine. And a few days later on a small ship in the Pacific, this couple spent the evening under candlelight, recalling highlights of a long shared life, but they also drank a toast to the good health of our family, who made, from vineyard to cellar, their favorite bottle of wine.

These images stay with you somewhere deep inside, and put a smile on your face at the most unexpected times.

16 ~ THE MULTI-GENERATIONAL FAMILY

*T*he Bartolommeis live at the head of the dirt road that dips and winds for a mile before ending at our house. Their house is called Caprili. It is ancient and rambling, especially since they added a new piece for the winery and another for the family of the elder son. At the heart of the house is a big courtyard shaded from the summer sun by trellised vines, leaving the stone pavement speckled with soft light. In the house, around the courtyard, live seven Bartolommeis spanning four generations, all of them working their vineyards and winery.

Although Tuscans live in clusters, they still cherish their independence, so the house has been converted into three apartments. In one lives the youngest, Giacomo, with his parents; in the next live his grandparents and his uncle Paolo; and on the ground floor Settimia, the great-grandmother, because after a long day in the vineyards or herding the pig through the woods where a carpet of acorns lies, she likes to be by herself in silence. She likes the ground floor with no stairs to climb, so she can save her strength for climbing ladders to pick fruit or olives.

A half mile up the road and a quarter mile up the hill, in a vast enchanted castle with a double courtyard, a chapel, and its own family vault, live three generations of Castellis; below them at Solderas' also three; and below us at Fattois' three again. Only we, refugees from another culture, with Buster now away at university, are down to just one. And even in merely practical terms, not to mention the constant joy and rich emotions that filled the house when he was there, his absence is felt every season, every day.

As with the family business, one tends to evaluate the pros and cons of multigenerational living in merely practical terms, and perhaps that is a good place to begin. There is a Tuscan saying that initially sounds callous: "Wear the old out first." Or, put crudely, the old work until the end. At all the houses around us, the oldest are first to rise, and even though they might slow with the years (Settimia is 84, Castelli is 85, and Soldera and Fattoi are in their mid seventies), it is their enormous zest for life, their sparkling eyes, their energetic gait, that seems to be the driving force at each and every house. And if you ask them, they will tell you they would not have it any other way. And so they shouldn't. Innumerable studies have shown that constant activity, both physical and mental, holds at bay an enormous number of deadly diseases, from heart disease and stroke to diabetes and Alzheimer's.

Just as important is the constant mental stimulation,

not only by the varied work I mentioned, but also by inter-action with the family, which keeps your mind sharp well into your years, so you remain interesting, entertaining, and hence sought-after company. And since everything you do is related in some detail to the family's daily life, your com-ments and input are of shared interest to all. And your alert-ness and wisdom, combined with the country's oral tradi-tion, most often makes you an engaging storyteller, adding even more to your social appeal.

It's not difficult to imagine the vitality that Ofelio feels returning from a hunt carrying a pheasant, or Settimia's self-esteem when she cooks the family's daily five-course meal or a feast for fifteen relatives and friends who come to help har-vest the grapes. And what a gift of fulfillment she receives with the sincere compliments paid after such meals.

How different all this is from North America's retire-ment villages, where only the movement of forced exercise interrupts the monotony of what can be called, without mal-ice, "artificial lives" in which the only shared interests are bodily functions and ailments.

~

One reason the revered Tuscan cuisine has survived through centuries is that the oldest in the house has always been there to cook. And by cooking I mean having the patience and pas-sion for sauces and stews that must simmer for hours, and meats that roast in wood ovens for the same, and pastas that take all morning to knead, roll, and slice. But only a small part of the secret that makes Tuscan cuisine so varied and savory is to be found in the kitchen. Just as with wine making—where only ten or fifteen percent of the outcome is determined in the cellars, the rest starting much farther back in the vineyards—cooking starts in the fields, the barnyard, and the vegetable gardens. The best of skills and intentions will not produce a great meal or great wine, unless what you put in the pot or barrel has been raised or grown with boundless love and care. The oldest generation appreciates that. They have, through long years of practice and observation, learned that there is not just one secret to cooking, or wine, or life, but myriad little things, all of which take time. And all their help, all their contribution, whether cooking or raising chickens or looking after young children with that infinite patience and dedication that only grandparents can provide, creates an atmosphere of security around the house, so the parents can more calmly tend to their own demanding daily lives.

It seems the older you get, the more you appreciate your family, so grandparents can act as a buffer between parents who, often confusing success with happiness, are often too busy to indulge children longing for nurture and contact. And how reassuring for children of all ages to know they're coming home not to an empty house but to one where there is always someone there to care and share a life.

It is this ever-present involvement of grandparents that produces such continuity in Tuscany, for children learn through effortless exposure to culinary skills, chores, and managing complex interactions with friends or members of the family. And here we should mention one of the least talked-about aspects of childrearing: physical affection, what we mistakenly abbreviate as "hugs". A few years ago bumper stickers appeared that asked, "Did you hug your kid today?" Not only is it frightening that we even had to ask, but worse is how pathetic little that hug or two is compared to the massive quantity of physical affection our children really need. Hugs, schmugs—we need smothering. And how much smothering? Judging by the average child, all we can get. Most grandparents are happy to be smothering machines.

~

Another great gift of grandparents is their calm, teaching children by example this most elusive but indispensable quality of life. In return, the spirit and zest of grandchildren energize the elders; it is an almost perfect symbiosis and constant exchange of exuberance and love. Again, what a far cry from both the elderly and the very young in our culture, ghettoized into their own age groups.

In merely practical terms, perhaps the middle generation benefits the most. Not only do they have built-in babysitters for the children, but many household chores, whether inside or out, are most often performed by the elders. In these days of endless after-school lessons and games, the role of chauffeur often falls on the elders. And since most Tuscans grow up with good exchange and support among family members, it is always reassuring for the middle generation to have the older one handy, if not for advice, then at least as someone who will listen. And as anyone who has had a good listener for a friend can tell you, a sympathetic ear is often enough to get you through the day. To grandparents' roles as babysitters, cooks, maids, and chauffeurs, you can also add analyst.

~

Tuscans provide for children no matter how old they are. A friend drew an interesting parallel between Tuscan and North American families: In America, if a child in his mid-twenties is still living in the family house, the neighbors shake their heads and ask, "What's wrong with that child?" In Tuscany, if the same child leaves the family home, the neighbors shake their heads and wonder, "What's wrong with that family?"

In fact, surveys show that 50 percent of all Tuscan males between twenty and thirty still live at home. And when they do decide to move, it is often into a home that has been provided by the family. And why not? Don't young couples have enough to confound them, enough to worry about? The marriage, the jobs, the children, without having to worry about the mortgage? The Tuscan solution is often the most simple: just as the friary we rebuilt was made of thirteen pieces, added bit by bit as needed through the years, so most Tuscans, when the time comes for their child to marry, simply try to add on to their house, whether in country or in town, whether it's a new addition or a conversion of a barn, stable, or garage. And if all else fails and there truly is no room, then the parents try to buy something nearby, hopefully within walking distance, so the family can be together at a moment's notice, to make running home to Mom or Grandma—or vice versa—an effortless enterprise.

Tuscan children, exposed to the limitless generosity of grandparents, learn the simple act of giving to the point of it being reflexive. So it's impossible to walk into a Tuscan house, even just to ask a simple question, without being insistently invited to sit down for a glass of wine or a glass of grappa, and to have at whatever time of day a little bite to eat. This constant giving and sharing permeates children. Buster has no grandparents, but the Fattois and the Paoluccis and Marina and Francesco made up for that lack many times over. He lived at their houses many an afternoon, always invited to the big midday meal, always fed and stuffed like a Christmas goose. And it stuck with him. Few things are as rewarding or as beautiful as to see Buster's face beaming with joy as he brings a little gift he made for Mom, or comes with some *porcini* or wild asparagus he found in the woods.

There is also the invisible gift of reassurance. When family troubles erupt, as they often do, with parents fighting, grandparents soften the impact with their consoling presence. And in the event of parental sickness or death, what can be more comforting than being shored by grandparental love?

The middle generation, too, receives emotional

rewards, and not just the obvious support in times of need but also the knowledge in the back of one's mind that the grandparents are there to look after the house and children. And if the children leave, whether for school or marriage, how nice to have someone to fill that empty nest.

The often boisterous, sometimes tumultuous, multi-generational family seems to provide enough emotion to satisfy most needs.

17 ~ GETTING A LIFE

With our North American values, we may bristle at the togetherness of Tuscan families and even communities. That's because we are accustomed to a fragmented society that not only separates rich from poor, but isolates us further into narrow segments by age. Segmentation, like urbanization, exists to bolster commerce. Marketers realized that the more they divide us from one another's nurturing company—the more they can make us feel isolated and lonely—the more we will shop to forget our loneliness. So we were divided into "marketable" segments that could be sold kiddie gyms, then teen phones, then retirement villages. The consumer culture reached its apex once we all believed that material possessions can substitute for a passionate human life; that happiness, fulfillment, love, and laughter would burst upon us as soon as we were awash in material goods. Little did we realize that the opposite is true.

And we prepare our children for the consumer life

from birth. We drown our children in physical comforts but deprive them of our love and our time. So instead of teaching them—not through lectures but by example—to value people, to cherish human company and friendship above all, we inadvertently teach them to value what they own. And instead of teaching them how to share, which Tuscans learn from birth through interdependence, we teach them how to hoard. And all their fine possessions leave them little room to imagine, almost no need to fantasize, and no need to invent. And that leaves us by and large with a legion of young who, bereft of affection and varied human company, are frighteningly homogenous in their lack of vision and dreams.

And when we inundate our children with possessions—toys, TV and myriad distractions—we bury one of life's great treasures: mystery. When, with well-intentioned kindness, we deluge them with electronic wonders—the blatant, the sensational—we numb them to the subtleties, not only of their fellow humans, but also of the natural world around them. Human behavior, as well as the miracles of ever-changing nature—mountains, woods, creeks, meadows, and bogs—hold little if any intrigue. Why would they? What fascinates instead is the new gadget and new gear. And since each gadget and gear is identical from coast to coast, and all entertainment is identical from coast to coast, we end up with a continent of clones, where individuality is no longer even rumor.

And while this life of joystick and remote control gives our children a sense of empowerment over their mechanical world, it doesn't encourage them to be pensive or insightful. It doesn't help them to be understanding or creative or even outrageous in real life, but how to follow step-by-step instructions, how to perfect hand-eye coordination, how to become fodder for the assembly line of life.

~

And with everyone busy X-boxing or Twittering or watching five hundred TV channels of their virtual world, who will take the time to understand humanity? Or help humanity, or even look at a simple human face? What chance does a human being who merely talks, smiles, and yodels now and then, stand against a screen that flashes, explodes, and crashes eleven times a second? And why have real friends with complex problems that may demand your time and love when you can click a mouse and find a dozen virtual ones a minute? Who needs real people when we have mechanical lovers and electronic friends?

One of the most insightful—and moving—comments on the subject comes from *The New Yorker*'s long-time television critic Nancy Franklin. She describes Barack Obama's inauguration as she watched it on her television through the day. She talks about the pomp, the crowds, the emotions, the adorable first daughters, the "hot and cool" Obamas during what may have been "the greatest day in American history." But she concludes thus:

"The morning after the Inauguration, something felt wrong to me. I was sad and unsettled, as if I'd had a bad dream. Later in the day, I realized how far away I'd felt from the events of the previous days. I'd seen Obama become President, verified that—*phew!*—it had actually happened, but I hadn't felt connected to it . . . I should have put the remote down and got myself to Washington and stood in the crowd, freezing and cheering, maybe even, for the first time, waving a flag. January 20th might have been the greatest day in my lifetime. By watching it on TV, I'd missed it."

~

Tuscans don't knowingly discourage this kind of virtual life, but they effortlessly furnish such an intense and humane real one, packed with real emotions—not all positive, but all of them filled with passion, whether sadness or happiness, love, fear, anger, or joy—that, even to the youngest, the superficial thrill of electronic distractions holds little lasting appeal. And when one has real friends in the family and community, the imaginary bond with strangers soon loses its luster. Just as Tuscans find industrial food revolting to the senses, so the shallow thrill of virtual friends seems to them but a sad substitute for real live flesh and blood. They have learned that a hundred of your very "best" Facebook friends aren't worth one by your side when you need him. And they seem to understand that when you live in electronic fantasy, you neglect the reality at hand. That attention, care, and emotion are often wasted on those whose life you influence not at all, robbing precious time from those who truly love you and rely for their happiness on your love and care.

18 ~ THE WRONG ROAD TAKEN

*O*ur drifting apart as a society was not accidental; we didn't just stumble onto a road streaming with material goods, we were led there by those we trusted—and we followed even though our common sense said "don't."

~

To the average Tuscan, politicians seem a curious species, as I found out ten years ago at the open-air market in our town of Montalcino, just days before George W. Bush was first elected.

The market of covered stalls descends from the ancient fortress (eleventh century), winds past the small park of pines (thirteenth century), extends up past the post office (day before yesterday), and ends in the tiny *piazza* below the Renaissance façade of the church of Sant'Agostino. It is a well-organized place. The first stalls have flowers and plants so that if you're in love you can just grab a bouquet and forget the rest because, for those in love, food and clothes have no meaning; or if you just want trays of seedlings for your *orto*, the vegetable garden, because you grow everything yourself, you can just load up and be on your way. Housewares come next because even if you grow all your own ingredients, sooner or later you'll need a frying pan; then shoes because they wear out soonest; then clothes of all kinds, with buxom mannequins in lacy black braziers and furry hats that Siberians wear when it's 60 below.

The best part of the market is under Sant'Agostino: the food. There are stalls with great rounds of *pecorino* cheese, and slabs of *prosciutto*, and strings of wild boar sausages harder than a rock, and roasted suckling pig on a spit, and great steaming *porchetta*, a huge hunk of roast pork stuffed with rosemary, sage, garlic and enough salt to cement shut the arteries of a rhinoceros.

Then there are three stands of fruits and vegetables. The first is owned by a frail older lady, and it's not really a stand but her husband's three-wheel motorbike dressed as a pick-up truck, with modest mounds of things they grew: still-soiled heads of garlic or onions, or clumps of sage, or bouquets of spinach or mounds of tomatoes of every shape and size. The other two stands are bigger, professional. One is informal, with things in wooden crates, the other more artistic, with everything in neat pyramids or circles.

The artistic *signora* seemed agitated that Friday morning. She piled her fruit with unusual aggression, and slammed down bunches of celery as if beating on a drum. I ordered a kilo of this and a kilo of that, but I couldn't resist:

"You're not happy today," I said. *"Che c'è?"*

She punched a turnip, then started wagging her hand. "Who would vote for a man like that?!" she blurted.

"Like what?"

"Like that man running for president. That Bush. I saw him on TV."

"And?"

"He's stupid."

"You understand English?" I asked, surprised.

"What English? I saw his eyes. I look at a turnip and I see a turnip. I look at a stupid and I see a stupid."

"He's not a genius," I admitted.

"He's *stupid!* And he wants to run a country?" she roared, and slapped a big ripe pumpkin. "I wouldn't let that man stack my tomatoes!"

She fell silent and gave me a bag of clementines.

"Your Berlusconi is not exactly Einstein," I smiled.

"Berlusconi is a clown. He's harmless. And *he* doesn't run the country; *we* run the country! But in America *that* will run the country."

I had to nod. She approved my answer and handed me some pears. I paid and started down the hill.

"Porca troia!" Pig sow, she swore, and slammed down her celery so hard it broke in two. She looked at it in disappointment, then yelled out to one and all, "Celery half price! Election special! "

~

Whereas ten years ago I thought her reaction extreme, standing now in the perfect storm of an imploding economy, crumbling environment, and our anxious, frantic lives, I must admit, with the benefit of hindsight, that the shattered celery was a colossal understatement.

While it's true that in those years we have achieved modern miracles with quantum leaps in science, technology, medicine and communication, we also seem to work more, commute more, strut but mostly fret more, eat more, get fat, feel bad, then diet more, sleep less, and divorce more, and we have replaced between-meal snacks with Valium and Malox. And all because we allowed the wrong guys to stack tomatoes.

Meanwhile, our hopes for a secure job, a safe hearth, and a happy family—in short, the American Dream, attainment of which seemed easy not long ago—has, for many, gone from a dream to just a memory.

And we were so busy following our leaders in a frantic rush to wealth and progress that we lost sight of simple joys, and neglected our friendships and our relationships, forgetting the most precious thing our race ever invented: each other's company.

Our millennia-old values such as honesty and responsibility, and goals like creating a better world for all, were by and large discarded, replaced by a culture that would die laughing at the old saying, "It's better to give than to receive."

Through it all, Tuscany has remained faithful to itself. Sure, it got a bit wealthier, but except in a few cases, only *piano, piano,* slowly, slowly. And the foundation of its daily life, the values of the close-knit community, the inviolable family, the respect for land, food, and each other, remained much the same.

~

I have always believed that behind every calamity hides opportunity. We may just be at that rare, cataclysmic moment when we have a chance to reflect, and perhaps create a new Renaissance.

With our limitless access to knowledge and information, and the all-too-painful awareness of what has gone awry, this might be the ideal time to re-examine our lives, and what really nourishes us: our jobs, homes, communities, relationships, schools, and even our food and entertainment. It might be the ideal time to move beyond what Bob Herbert of *The New York Times* called "the nauseating idea that the essence of our culture and the be-all and end-all of the American economy is the limitless consumption of trashy consumer goods." And it might be the perfect time to find true security and lasting joy—that, which in life fulfills us, makes us proud to be human. It might be a good time to build a humane, enduring culture like the Tuscans'.

This is not a time for doom and gloom. We should be thrilled—as thrilled as those who began the Renaissance after the Dark Ages. And grateful—as grateful as the London schoolboy who, after a night of blitzkrieg, comes out of the bomb shelter and, with his books on his back, trudges off to school—only, rounding the corner, he sees his schoolhouse reduced to ruins. His face brightens, he throws up his arms, and, bursting with irrepressible joy, he yells out: "Thank you Adolf!!"

Who Let the Ladder Fall?

There's an old Tuscan saying, "Once the ladder falls, everyone knows what advise to give," but then, hindsight is still better than no sight at all.

At first glance it might seem a formidable task to try to reweave the web of our existence—economy, environment, and quality of life—but it gets easier when we realize that the original weaver of the web was us.

All of us leapt with both feet into the get-rich-quick fantasies of Wall Street's "magical thinking," which is "the tendency to believe that *wishing* it makes it so." And we never allowed our romp through Fantasyland to be interrupted by thoughtful voices like that of Nobel Prize-winning economist Paul Krugman, who admonished us for years for spending habits modeled after the drunken sailor.

We abandoned all common sense and went on a buying binge. We longed for everything ever produced and were willing to do anything—no matter how harmful or even self-destructive—to get it. We adopted as our anthem Cole Porter's *Anything Goes*.

And *everything* went.

First Enron, then Lehman Brothers, then Wall Street, then our 401Ks, then the Big Three automakers, and finally our jobs. They all went in what seemed a silent conspiracy that created bubble after fantasy bubble, the last one ending with the devastation of the American Dream, our home. To paraphrase another Tuscan saying, "If all idiots wore white caps, the world would look like a giant flock of geese."

So we willingly forgot that for generations the value of our homes rose slowly but steadily because, as the population grew, so did demand for houses. This dependable rise was helped by prudent bankers, who gave mortgages to those with proven credit, reliable income, and a down payment—"prime" customers, those with a high likelihood of paying a loan back.

But our bankers put common sense aside. When they ran out of primes they lunged at the sub-primes: those with no steady job, no credit, not even a down payment. The thinking was—if there was any—that if the sub-prime defaulted on his mortgage, he could simply sell. But the question no one answered, or worse, no one asked, was, "sell to *whom?*" Since the primes all had houses, as now did the sub-primes, who was there *more* jobless, *more* savings-less, *more* credit-less to sell to? The homeless? Preschoolers? The unborn?

Just asking.

Unfortunately, our whirlwind lives with forever-longer commutes and forever-longer working hours left us little time for thorough discussion or even contemplation. So from the thirty-second news sound bites we concluded that the value of our houses was doubling by the day. We were, at least on paper, unimaginably rich. Armed with the Keynesian dogma that no one outside a lunatic asylum would ever just "hold" money, we bit.

Boy, did we bit.

Many of us went willingly to the banks to retrieve our equity, while others had to be coaxed. Alex Kotlowitz wrote that in Cleveland, "mortgage brokers would cruise neighborhoods, looking for houses with old windows or a leaning porch, something that needed fixing. They would then offer to arrange financing to pay for repairs. Many of those deals were too good to be true, and interest rates ballooned after a short period of low payments. Suddenly burdened with debt, people began to lose homes they had owned free and clear."

The most horrific case was that of Addie Polk of Akron, Ohio. A widow at the age of 90, she found herself in foreclosure about to be forced from the home she lived in for forty years. As deputies knocked on her door with eviction papers in hand, she shot herself in the chest. Addie Polk, who once had her house paid for, was talked into a mortgage.

It is impossible to imagine any of this happening in a closely-knit society in which relatives, friends, and neighbors look out for each other and are involved in constant encounters and exchanges—and, just as important, where everyone knows the banker and vice versa. Doubts would have arisen early and if a scam were discovered, the scammer would have been persuaded to stop by friends and relations using an age-old Tuscan argument involving a length of piano wire, some dangling, and his balls. Or, as Nebbia once said, "Fool me once, shame on you. Fool me twice and you'll sing soprano."

~

There's an old Tuscan saying, "He who listens too much to the brains of others will soon lose his own." We appear to be listening to others more and more.

It seems we have lost faith in ourselves to analyze and judge, so we turn to others, politicians and businesspeople, to lead us. When they turn out to be self-serving or fraudulent, we seem surprised. But we shouldn't be, because we might just have followed leaders who were suffering from an affliction first popular in the nineteenth century: "moral insanity." The modern term is psychopathy. While psychopaths can be charming and intelligent, they are also "self centered, dishonest, irresponsible, emotionally shallow, and lacking insight." The psychiatrist Hervey Cleckley argued that the individualistic, winner-take-all aspect of American culture nurtures psychopathy. And professor Robert Hare wrote, "The most agreeable vocation for psychopaths is business . . . with its ruthlessness, lack of social conscience, and single minded devotion to success."

It seems plain that our lack of insight and social conscience was exactly what allowed our planet to be degraded to the point where we can no longer be sure exactly what we will be passing on to future generations, "if," as Nick Paumgarten of *The New Yorker* coldly remarked, "there turn out to be any."

~

Even though almost all respected scientists agreed years ago that our lifestyle was the principal cause of global warming, as recently as early 2008 President Bush remained a skeptic, and that same year the chief executive of General Motors called global warming "a crock of shit." And none of us went to them with baseball bats and bricks to explain how things really stood. Left untethered, Detroit's Big Three produced enormous vehicles with enormous gas consumption—and even more enormous profit margins—while they brainwashed us into believing that we were uncool lest we drove things that were, until the year before, reserved for hauling hogs.

The construction industry, seeing that size mattered if you wanted mega profits, followed suit with enormous houses. And, inexplicably, previously sensible people who had lived comfortably and happily in the cozy togetherness of modest homes felt suddenly compelled to live in giant barns where it would often take a search party to find one another. The rest of our world went similarly mad producing—if not "super-sized," then at least super new—every trinket and gadget imaginable to man. While our brains took the decade off, our feet went on marching relentlessly to the mall. And we ate endlessly and much until half the population looked as if it had swallowed an air hose. Even though our belts, closets, and U-Store-Its were already bursting, armed with home equity loans and plastic, we continued the shopping spree of the millennium.

We bought boom boxes and then iPods, flat screens and DVD's, instamatics, Veg-O-Matics, popcorn makers, muffin bakers, machines to mow the lawn, fry a prawn, shear the dog, saw a log, blow snow, leaves, hair, or air; we bought gear to barbecue a chicken, broil it, roast it, deep-fry it or toast it or put it in the Microwave and blow it to the moon; bought chemicals to calm our fits, dry our pits, expand our tits, we became modern Hurdy-Gurdy men, with electronics dangling from every orifice and limb. Had our lives become so meaningless that we had to fill each moment with a toy?

So we ended up in what the media has titled the Age of Anxiety. Little wonder. Who wouldn't be anxious leading a life that made no sense?

19 ~ YOUR OWN TUSCANY

If ever there were a chance to rekindle our spirit of adventure, and change our lives dramatically for the best, it has to be these times of social and financial limbo. As the old saying goes, "Strike while the iron is hot." And perhaps we can build an even better Tuscany than the Etruscans; after all, they had but crude tools, stones, and mud, whereas we have not just iPhones but also claw hammers and even Elmer's glue.

So what's holding us back?

Asked where we would like to wake up, would any of us really say, "Stuck on a freeway, drinking can't-remember-what from a paper cup, on the way to a job titled, 'May not be there tomorrow'"? If that's your answer, R. I. P.

But if you say, "In a little house with a garden in a small town or the country," then read on, because there's emotional buttressing waiting up ahead.

And there is no need to actually move to Tuscany, because what we seek—economic security, emotional calm, diversity of work, and living among friends and family amidst beauty and nature—is probably waiting just over the hill. Unless you live in Hoboken, in which case, forget it.

So what are you waiting for? Why not dump the house—it's worth less than the mortgage, anyway—pack up the kids, kiss the boss goodbye, and head for the country?

For security and flexibility, nothing can surpass the country family. As social theorist John Berger wrote, "It is the only class of people with a built-in resistance to consumerism," and hence a built-in resilience to unemployment, recessions, inflation, and deflation. It's hard to imagine a tighter or more stable social unit than a country family and its neighbors, all of whom share the same problems, hopes, harvests, and droughts, not to mention the vicious case of poison ivy when you all sit in the grass together in shorts.

After a lifetime of research in both psychology and anthropology, Carl Jung found the hamlet or village to be the ideal human habitation. So did Lewis Mumford, who spent the last decades of his life in upstate New York in his beloved hamlet of Amenia.

But country life is not for the faint of heart. You will need imagination, clear thinking, a strong back, much spirit—preferably 80 proof—and some good old-fashioned common sense. You first objection might be that you don't know a tree from a lamp pole, but that bit of self-knowledge is a good place to start. There's more help and advice available out there than you care to have. If you're stuck, just look around or go visit and ask questions. It's the best way to meet the neighbors, and people love to help. And the more you can learn from those around you, especially those who have lived on and worked the land, know the secrets, and know the seasons, the more confident and comfortable you will become.

Or if you don't want to strike out on your own, take your best friends along. Those who work the hardest and grumble the wittiest will make first-class country neighbors. The Abbotts and Keiths near Barrie, Ontario did just that: with help from their friends, they started their own hamlet, one of many that have mushroomed in Canada and Denmark.

The Abbotts and Keiths found a ninety-four-acre piece of land, part marginal farmland, part woods, where they now, with seven other families—all friends—"share ownership of the land, gardens, orchards, a couple of old tractors and even a flock of thirty chickens . . . yet each owning an acre with a custom-built house where privacy is respected."

Acquiring the property in common enabled the group not only to get the sizable acreage, which none could have afforded on its own, but also to buy in an area that still offers large tracts of land, where the price per acre was significantly less.

Each owner designed his or her own house, and all paid attention to energy conservation. So one house is built right into a hillside with much glazing on the side exposed to the sun, another is heated by an enormous fireplace that holds heat overnight, while the Abbotts' 1,600-square-foot home is heated largely by solar energy; in their severe winter climate, they get by with but a single cord of wood.

~

The physical aspects of new hamlets are always of prime concern. Most group their houses to create a more intimate community and to leave the rest of the land wide open and free. The houses are laid out in circles or other clusters, shutting out streets and cars and allowing for the reinvention of such highly social traditions as the village green and the village pond, both of them marvelous places for children to play freely and the community to informally gather.

The Barrie hamlet decided to own machinery like lawn mowers, rototillers, and tractors in common to share cost and maintenance, yet the greatest rewards of sharing were the social gains. Each family built its house with the help of friends. They also worked together building a common pond that irrigates the gardens and serves as a swimming hole in summer and skating rink in winter. They even make maple syrup together, and put up each other's overflow of guests.

Some hamlets also work orchards and fields together. This makes practical sense, for the single best spot can be found to suit each crop, but more important, working together strengthens the community, and few things are more enjoyable than the multitude of celebrations growing things can bring. And the best part is that these will be about your talent, *your* work, with friends who are just as much a part of it as you.

Critics will say that we have evolved far beyond simple

country life, that we are too modern. Yet as Jung said, "The psyche is not of today. It reaches back to prehistoric ages. Has man really changed in ten thousand years? Have stags changed their antlers in this short lapse of time?"

And it is also true that the new hamlets are tiny, hence, no matter how fast they spread, it will take time for them to alter society. But when we live in a world as uncertain as ours, where we seem to pile one economic, social, and environmental blunder atop another, then the new hamlets may be the first light of dawn at the end of a long and increasingly scary night.

~

The wisest thing Tuscany has taught me is to be content, even thrilled, with the basic things in life. Of course I had loved my "basic" houseboat days, and the months Candace and I bummed around in our van, and the years we gunk-holed on the sailboat; yet I still often shock myself at random intervals with an irrepressible urge to suddenly want "more." That's when Tuscany steps in with a visit to the neighbors, and I calm down again.

Contentment with life is contagious in Tuscany.

~

Human contentment seems to require very little: a roof, a good meal on the table, fresh air, and a secure family and good friends in a true community. Throw in excellent public education, anxiety-free health care and decent public transportation—okay, and maybe a cellar full of wine, olive oil, and garlic—and you'll have yourself a society that, if Tuscany is any proof, produces alert, intelligent, independent, morally strong, and socially responsible people. Since contentment seems so achievable, shouldn't that be society's main goal? Shouldn't it be chiseled into every constitution?

Of course, Tuscans have a big jump on us, because they had the good sense to preserve the miraculously beautiful landscape and towns they inherited. The most stringent of laws have kept Tuscany from being carpet-bombed by urban sprawl like California, or even worse, Florida, where Doug Bennet of the *St. Petersburg Times* looked out over the half-completed, half-abandoned subdivisions that stretched without parks, without social centers, without a heart to the horizon. "Stucco ghettos," he said. "This is the epicenter of everything that's bad in America."

~

Would the world not be a better place if we could, like many Tuscans, bequeath our children a piece of fertile land, a modest house, basic life skills, and a tightly knit community that gives us identity, self respect and pride?

We could, once again, become like the truly democratic corners of 1800s America, where, as de Tocqueville wrote, "Each citizen developed his civic mores informally, through conversations on street corners or in the square; in the day-to-day encounters in the shops; on the walks that took him past public buildings and houses of worship and settings of great natural beauty—that took him, if only for a moment, out of his private self."

We could make our cities livable again. As their population is reduced by the exodus to small towns, villages, hamlets, and the land, they could reorganize into livable villages themselves. Such a transformation is proposed for Flint, Michigan, where partially abandoned neighborhoods are to be demolished and the population condensed around stores and services. Parts of a formerly highly industrial city would be returned to the forest primeval.

In our new villages, the car would be just an ugly memory; mothers could safely push their babies' strollers to the local shops and parks; the air would be as clean and quiet as in the country. What manufacturing remained would produce everything with extreme thought and care, backed by an unconditional five-year guarantee, or better yet, one for a lifetime; where the city would be a center for the best culture could offer, not a place for the richest and gaudiest to preen and strut their wares.

Obsession with possessions would die from lack of interest, as soon as those obsessed were relegated from national idols to unfortunate clowns. It can happen. It happened with smoking.

Some may say that all this is just a romantic's musings on a sunny summer's day. I don't think so. There seems to be no great chasm between our machine-run, mass-produced urban world and a humane, quality-centered one. Indeed, the major difference seems to be that in urban life we confine ourselves to performing often hated jobs just to house and feed ourselves, and be able on our two-week holidays to rush out and pay for all the things we love: gardening, tinkering, visiting, crafting, gathering, and celebrating—all the things that, in a reasonable village, are the fundamental, sustaining, daily parts of life.

~

A new eco-city, Dongtan, is designed and slated to open for Expo 2010 on an island near Shanghai. Burkhard Bilger wrote that it is to be self sufficient in water, energy, and most foods, with mainly foot or bicycle transport. It is to contain farmland, parkland, and even wetlands. It is billed as the sustainable city of the future. Bilger's closing comment was, "It's not so different from the towns Europeans built a thousand years ago."

Most of us are too restless to wait for a Dongtan to rise near us. Rightfully so. Then we can do what our friend Fred Smith did in the Gulf Islands.

When he was forty-four, working in a gravel pit doing everything from driving machinery to repairing it, Fred decided he had had enough. On a small peninsula on the shores of Welcome Bay, he got himself five acres. It was covered with evergreens, had a small gravel beach, and the view across the sound held not only islands but also snow-capped mountains.

On weekends and on holidays he cleared a spot for the house and for a meadow to raise a handful of sheep, which would supply lamb for meat and wool that his wife Vi would knit into sweaters. He stripped and cleaned the logs and stacked them to season. A year later, he started his 800-square-foot house. He built the foundation with stones from the fields, notched and veed the logs, and, since they were small, he set them in place with the help of an A-frame and Vi. The cedar shingles for the roof he split from driftwood he found on shore. The stones for the fireplace he hauled up from the beach. He had a small local sawmill cut some logs to planks, which he used for flooring, doors, cabinets, and windows. Much of the furniture he made from tree limbs.

When he was forty-eight, Fred Smith quit his job. He had no pension. After paying twenty-seven years into unemployment insurance, he received only one week's check, with the explanation that he was moving to an area where there were no jobs to be found. They were on their own. They moved into the log house. Vi said she'd try living in the boonies for a year. That was thirty-two years ago. In those thirty-two years, they have left Welcome Bay for only short holidays.

They thrive by their wits and the work of their own hands. They sell fruit and vegetables and eggs and chickens at the weekly farmers' market, Vi knits sweaters to order, Fred helps neighbors on occasion with everything from building sheds to repairing wooden boats, and he fishes and catches crabs. On a spit far from the house they built a tiny cabin to let out to summer tourists, and they cleared three spots on shore for families to camp—in tents. Their expenses are few.

They grow everything they eat and preserve almost all the things they grow, and they have re-invented things one sees but in old movies: sewing on buttons instead of throwing out a shirt, darning holes in clothes or making them from scratch, making toys for grandchildren and presents for their friends.

They are absolutely independent and completely secure. And if I had to name the happiest man I know, Fred Smith would be it.

It can be done.

20 ~ THE CYPRESSES
OF TUSCANY

*T*he guard tower where I write was built in 1511, a mere nineteen years after Columbus set foot in the new world. The date is etched with long, elegant numbers into a cornerstone. The tower is on a hillside, so I can look out across the valley full of knolls, over the olive grove and vineyard we planted, at a clump of dark cypresses rising against the sky. Among them, in a walled-in graveyard, is a tiny chapel. You have to walk up close to see its doors permanently ajar, the grass around it tall and tangled, with here and there a rusted iron cross. If you lean down you can see some fallen tombstones, so old and weathered that you cannot read a name. The silence and the cypress shadows make this a good spot on a hot summer day for sitting in solitude.

The cypresses have been here for centuries. There are two other such clumps in our valley, one next to the hilltop hamlet of Camigliano, another at an abbey that dominates a crest. And you can see them readily against the pale wheat fields of June, or the red vines of October, or the dusting of snow that falls in December like a benediction. Whether picking olives, pruning vines, hoeing vegetables, or cutting hay, when you look up the cypresses catch your eye. I have always wondered why. Were they planted by the church to act as dark candles pointing at the Heavens? To assure you that no matter how hard your toil, Heaven is waiting as your final prize? Or were they planted by the *contadini* who, with their families, worked the land, to remind them at each glance that the cold marble was waiting, and you'd better enjoy this earthly life each day while you can? Knowing Paolucci, who would interrupt any work to talk, or Marina's welcoming smile, or Francesco's crushing handshake and insistent invitation to come in for a while, a glance at those cypresses has meant the same through the centuries: it's never too soon to stop with a friend for a glass of wine.

APPENDIX

*P*ino Luongo, a fiftieth generation Tuscan, has been feeding our family for over 20 years. Not only did he teach Candace how to cook, but much more importantly taught her to love cooking. And he taught her to improvise and be creative in the kitchen, giving her a first sampling of Tuscan self-confidence and independence.

His passionate approach to life, people, and food is the very essence of the Tuscan way. He cooks not with a measuring cup and spoon but with all his senses, and he invites, indeed compels, those who read him to do the same. His knowledge and his insights into Tuscan life add an invaluable dimension to this book. His anecdotes capture our imagination like only those of a born-and-raised Tuscan can.

The following is excerpted from his culinary classic *A Tuscan in The Kitchen.* He is currently feeding his grateful clientele at his restaurant Centolire, in uptown Manhattan.

A TUSCAN IN THE KITCHEN
Pino Luongo

My relationship with the food of Tuscany is very simple: it was the food of my childhood. I grew up loving the countryside of Tuscan cuisine and the way people used the land. Tuscany is a region of peasants who have always worked the land, growing their own vegetables, keeping their own animals. They have never been a rich people, but they have always found inventive ways to cook something wonderful with the things they had.

We say that if you grow up, as I did, in a family in which every resource has to be used 100 percent, you become an imaginative cook so that, one day, if your life improves—even if you can afford to buy expensive things—you still have the ability to create something special from the few ingredients you have.

Tuscan cuisine gives you this chance. It encourages you to adapt and improve on the original, because Tuscan food has never become an institution. It has always been open to the personal efforts and imagination that make better-tasting dishes. In Tuscany we don't want chefs cooking for us—we want Mamma!

Tuscans believe that the best food you can eat is in your own home. But cooking shouldn't be an ordeal. It should be the pleasure of creating something you want to share with the people you care about most.

When you stock a Tuscan kitchen you need to have a certain vision more than you need advice. Think about a very tiny Tuscan lady who, in her kitchen, has stored enough pasta, olive oil, dried beans, canned tomatoes, garlic, and so on to be ready for any event.

With not too much strength in her arms, she has carried a grocery bag and gone out for a walk to see what's available at the local market. "Oh, it's Thursday. I'm going to stop at the fish market because they have fresh fish today." And then she picks a few anchovies to make with garlic, parsley, olive oil, and white wine. Next, she asks the butcher, "You have a new pig today, yes? Give me four chops. I'm coming back in five minutes." She goes to the poultry shop and gets four or five eggs. Then she goes to the vegetable market. "It's May. You have any good cherries?" "Sure, I've got cherries." She also picks up rucola, cucumbers, tomatos. On the way home, she buys a loaf of bread at the bakery. And she heads toward home, content in the knowledge that she has had her daily walk and completed her duties.

So keep this vision in mind, even if you don't live in a small hill town in Tuscany.

To make life easier, I've divided the ingredients by the place they're kept in any Tuscan kitchen. Items that can be stored without refrigeration because they are not perishable are listed under Pantry (La Dispensa). Ingredients that require refrigera-

tion are listed under *Cold Storage* (La Cantina). *At this point, if you have a pantry and a refrigerator well-stocked with those items used repeatedly in these recipes, all you need to do is buy these few fresh items that the recipes list under Market* (Il Mercato).

Let's talk about some of the most important elements of Tuscan cooking.

Olive Oil

The classification of "extra virgin" is the most important consideration when you're shopping for olive oil. It's a guarantee that the olives where hand picked from the trees and the oil has been pressed in the old system, with stone wheels and without the use of heat. Also, look on the label to see if the olives were grown and the oil produced and bottled on the same estate. This assures you of extreme quality control.

Olive oil can be used for cooking, of course, but its main purpose is to flavor, so it's best left the way it is—raw, natural. Olive oil can be added to top off a soup or a stew— it's like a heavenly coat.

Fresh-squeezed olive oil, when it is totally unfiltered and nothing has been added, is the best natural medicine in the world. It makes the intestines function better; it's also good for the liver and pancreas. When you know you're going to drink a lot, just take a spoonful of olive oil and you won't have a hangover.

Odori

The foundation of many Tuscan dishes, such as soups, sauces, and stews, is *odori*—a mixture of finely chopped red onions, celery, carrots, parsley, and sometimes garlic in any combination you want. To make *odori*, first dampen the bottom of a pan with olive oil and then lightly cover it with the chopped vegetables. When you look inside the pan, you'll see a beautiful, colorful combination of orange carrots, light green celery, dark green parsley, and red onions. Sauté the vegetables over medium heat until they turn blond from cooking and the oil has been absorbed. Then continue with the necessary steps to complete whatever soup, stew, or sauce you're planning to make.

Garlic

Garlic is something you always want to eat, but you never want to smell like. The power of garlic excels in certain dishes like Spaghetti con Aglio, Olio, e Peperoncino or Fettunta, but in most other dishes, once the garlic has been browned, get rid of it, especially if you are preparing something delicate. The garlic flavor should be there, but not there.

A Note About Garlic: In most recipes in which garlic is used, it is first smashed with the heel of your hand or the flat side of a knife.

Herbs

I suggest that you get familiar with different herbs—their tastes, their effects on certain dishes, and the way they react in sauces. Then you won't have to limit yourself to rosemary with fish, or sage with game, or bay leaves with red meat. I make all kinds of dishes with all kinds of herbs.

My favorite common herbs are sage, basil (always fresh), rosemary, tarragon, thyme (always fresh), and bay leaves.

The peasant in Tuscany has always had a secret way of using herbs, and those herbs can change a dish dramatically. No matter what, even if the family were starving to death, and a dish were made from the poorest ingredients, the peasant always added the final touch—the particular taste of aromatic herbs.

If you want, you can grow herbs yourself in pots on a sunny windowsill in winter, or outside on a terrace in summer. Although some herbs are good dried—bay leaves and oregano for instance—sage and rosemary are much better fresh. And with thyme, there is a big difference between fresh and dried.

In my restaurant I keep herbs in quantity. I always buy pounds of everything. But even if you buy fresh herbs and dry them yourself, they are still useful.

Not all herbs are available during the winter, so it's smart to grow or buy fresh herbs in season to keep in your pantry for the winter. If you dry sage, oregano, rosemary, tarragon, thyme, and bay leaves at home they will turn out 100 percent better than if you buy them dried at the supermarket.

Tomatoes

I use fresh salad (beefsteak) or plum tomatoes in salads only when they're in season, and I only use fresh plum tomatoes for sauces and stews when they are very ripe.

If they are picked early in the season when they are still slightly orange in color and not too juicy, they are excellent in salads. Later, when they are very ripe, I make them into a Filetto di Pomodoro, which I use in certain dishes such as fresh pasta or the tiny *tagliolini*. When the tomato is so fresh, so tasty, and so ripe, you want to cook it as little as possible. If you're making a stewed dish like an ossobuco, which you cook for a long time, leave the skins on the tomatoes because actually they add extra taste and texture to the dish.

As soon as the season is over, it's not a bad idea to consider using just the good-quality imported canned tomatoes.

Pasta

I suggest you buy imported dry pastas, since they are easier to cook al dente than the domestic varieties. When you cook, it is important to start checking for doneness after about three or four minutes. When you bite into pasta, your teeth will tell you if it's done. Among the fresh pastas, the most commonly used in Tuscany are *tagliatelle*—a flat, thin noodle—

and *tagliolini,* which is even thinner. Fresh pasta is as important in Tuscan cooking as dry pasta because it is good with gamy and complicated sauces.

Bread

Whether Tuscan bread is made with whole wheat or white flour, it is unsalted. Centuries ago, Tuscany was such a poor country that many people couldn't afford to pay the tax levied on salt. Necessity became a tradition when it was found that the absence of salt enhanced without altering the flavor of food served with this bread.

A Note About Bread: Any time bread is mentioned, I mean a loaf of crusty peasant bread.

Beans

The urge to eat beans is so innate in the Tuscan people that they are used in every season, whether fresh or dried, in salads, soups, stews, or with roasts. In Tuscan cooking the most frequently used dried beans are cannellini beans, red beans, lentils, chick-peas, and lima beans. The fresh beans we like are red-eyed beans, fava beans, and all the shell beans that are fresh in summer.

The Essence of Tuscan Cooking

Ingredients are the essence of Tuscan cooking. The way a dish turns out depends much more on the ingredients you buy than on your cooking technique. Once you get the freshest ingredients, most of the important work has been done. In Tuscany, the farmer, the fisherman, and the hunter have more power over the table than the chef.

In Tuscany, we go to the market, see what looks the best, and plan our meal around these things, instead of deciding ahead of time what we want for dinner. Don't buy food that comes in plastic, already cut up. Instead, shop where you can touch the vegetables, look at them; where you can see the fish as it comes from the sea—it's color, the gills, the eyes— and smell it to see if it's fresh. It's nice to discover this way of shopping which adds pleasure to how you think and feel about preparing a meal.

And forget about amounts and cooking times when you use this book. I'll help you understand that in your own kitchen you have all the freedom in the world to do exactly what you want, and the best way to arrive at solutions is through common sense.

You'll also know from the name of the recipe which ingredients are going to dominate the dish, so buy more of that ingredient. You know if you're making soft-shell crab soup that the main ingredient is crabs. The taste and whole personality of the dish is determined by how one or two ingredients dominate the others, but even these proportions can be varied. In Tuscan cooking, you never find a cook who tells you, "This is it, this is the only way to make this dish." Instead, you always hear, "This is the way we make it; this is one of the ways we enjoy it." If you cook according to your own impulse, probably you will discover something about the way you like to cook.

Don't think that if you're given exact quantities and cooking times everything will turn out better. Sometimes it's the level of heat you use or the size of the pan that changes a dish. In between starting and finishing the dish, there are so many decisions you can make that if you follow a recipe given in tablespoons and minutes you'll just lose your freedom. And, finally, I don't give exact times for cooking, either. Instead I give an approximate time to start checking the dish to see if it's done. Why? First, an exact time doesn't exist. Second, there is a way to understand when food is ready that has nothing to do with the clock. Look at what's in the pan. See if it's getting too dry; smell it, penetrate it with a fork to see how tender it is. If you notice that it's a little too pink, cook it some more. If it's too dry, add more liquid. It's logical.

Recipes

Fettunta
Toasted Garlic Bread

Throughout history, parts of Tuscany have been overrun by bandits, floods, the government, and the papacy. Peasants knew what it meant not to have food—to have only bread to eat for days and weeks and months. In the early part of the century, the peasants went on a general strike to protest their treatment by the wealthy landowners. They just stopped working, all of them. It was probably during this period that Fettunta (in Tuscany, a slice of toasted garlic bread, wet with oil) was invented as the only way to survive the months of food shortages.

One thing the peasants had was flour, so they made a very simple bread of flour and water. The other thing they had was a very heavy, unfiltered olive oil, which the rich people, with their fine tastes, rejected. In the beginning, Fettunta was simply bread brushed with olive oil and salt, and then toasted. Then the peasants started to add garlic and, once in a while, some tomatoes. The big difference is that today we make Fettunta to enjoy it, but at that time the peasants made it to survive.

You can't make Fettunta with pre-sliced, plastic-wrapped bread. You have to use simple white Italian bread with a good crust.

Pantry: Olive oil, salt, black pepper
Cold Storage: Garlic
Market: Good Italian bread, sliced

Toast the bread and scrape a clove of garlic over one side of each slice. As you scrape, the garlic will disintegrate and release its pulp and juice into the bread. Sprinkle bread with olive oil.

In your home, it's nice if you serve plain toasted bread and on the table put cloves of garlic, a bottle of good olive oil, and salt and pepper. Each person scrapes as much garlic as he or she wants over the toasted bread and then puts on the olive oil, salt, and pepper.

Crostini Alla Fiorentia
Chicken Liver Pâté, Florentine-Style

My grandfather was 100 percent Florentine, like the fifty generations before him. His wife used to make chicken liver crostini, and I remember asking him, "Why, when we have this at your house, is the bread so soft? It's different from the crostini of my mother." He told me that in Florence they soften the bread in hot chicken broth before they put the pâté on top. If you dip hard bread in broth quickly, just long enough to moisten it, it doesn't get mushy or fall apart. This is a Florentine way of using stale bread.

I love this recipe because I love sharp tastes. Have this beautiful crostini with a slice of prosciutto and a bottle of fresh, young white wine, still sparkling a bit. Find a patio overlooking Florence, sit down, and forget about the rest of the world.

Pantry: Olive oil, capers, finely chopped, anchovies, finely chopped, salt, black pepper.
Cold Storage: Butter, chicken broth, fresh parsley, chopped (optional)
Market: Chicken livers (1 per person), fresh Italian bread, sliced

Sauté chicken livers over medium heat in equal amounts of butter and olive oil. Chop well, mix with capers and anchovies, and season with salt and pepper. Return to the pan and stir in a very little broth. Purée everything until it is the consistency of a thick paste. Serve warm or at room temperature on fresh bread. Sprinkle chopped parsley over the top if you want.

Porcini Alla Griglia
Grilled Porcini Mushrooms

It's best to serve a grilled porcini alone, because its taste is so strong and so full of personality that it doesn't need any help. It's the most egocentric mushroom you can find. It doesn't want anything next to it on the plate. It's so meaty and mellow, it's considered like a steak in its taste and richness. The only thing I would serve with a grilled porcini is a great bottle of red wine. That's the obligation. Just sharpen your tongue, because the taste is unbelievable. I could eat porcini three times a day.

Pantry: Olive oil, salt, black pepper
Market: Fresh porcini mushroom

Remove the caps of the mushrooms and reserve the stems for another use. Lightly oil the caps and place them on a grill or in the broiler like upside-down umbrellas. When half cooked, they will feel spongy and release some water when you press them gently. Turn them over and continue to cook until tender but still firm. Drizzle with olive oil and season with salt and pepper.

The Soups of Bread and Fantasy

Pasta and soup are eaten in every part of Italy, but in Tuscany, soup comes first in importance and then pasta. Soup appears on the table at least once a day and is considered as essential as any other course.

Tuscans like their soup rich and thick—with or without bread. Bread was the one element always present in the Tuscan kitchen, but fantasy raised a simple peasant soup to the level of culinary art. Bread may have filled the stomach, but Tuscan imagination provided the good taste. Today when you eat a bread soup in Tuscany you know that you are eating an original peasant dish. But even if the soup is without bread, it will still represent the Tuscan approach of combining many flavors into one satisfying spoonful.

The Bread Soups

Ribollita is an example what people ate many years ago in the area of Montalcino that have one thing in common: they are called zuppe di pane—bread soups. Bread, a main ingredient, satisfied hunger, and the remaining ingredients provided good taste, moistness, and fragrance. These soups are thicker and richer than the liquid soups most people are used to.

Ribollita
"Overcooked" Bread and Vegetable Soup

The Ribollita most often found in Tuscany includes beans and purple cabbage. The other vegetables vary according to the season and the mood of the cook. The following is the version I grew up with. Sprinkle extra olive oil in each bowl and serve the soup with raw, chilled scallions. A bite of scallion adds a sharp taste to each spoonful of soup.

Pantry: Olive oil, canned tomatoes smashed in their own juice, partially cooked cannellini beans, salt, black pepper, odori.
Cold Storage: Potatoes, cut into chunks.
Market: Zucchini (thinly sliced), cauliflower (cut in pieces), coarsely chopped cabbage (white and purple), chopped Swiss chard, spinach, bread (cut in chunks)

Heat the olive oil in a large pot and add the odori. Sauté over medium heat and, once the odori is soft, add the tomatoes, fresh vegetables, potatoes, cannellini beans, and just enough water to cover. Let them cook slowly until they are completely mushy. Season with salt and pepper. Take the soup off the heat, and add the bread and enough olive oil to flavor. Let the soup cool to allow the flavors to combine; it can even remain the refrigerator overnight. Put the mixture back on the heat and let it cook slowly for at least 30 minutes. Ribollita means "overboiled," so it is impossible to cook this soup too long.

Polenta
Cornmeal Mush, Tuscan Style

In the late nineteenth century in Tuscany, there was a malaria epidemic in Maremma, and government officials in bordering areas were authorized to destroy food and burn shacks where people had died. If you look carefully at paintings of Tuscany showing peasant food before that time, you see bread on the table, but after that if you see something yellow in the middle of the table, it's usually polenta. Tuscany was so poor that bread became the food of the rich and polenta the food of the poor.

Polenta can be a substitute for pasta or bread. It can be soupy like cornmeal mush or stiff like cornbread. I make it the first way once in a while for myself and eat it with sausage sautéed with tomatoes for another very strong dish. With a good bottle of wine, who's going to bother you? You're through for the day.

Pantry: Yellow cornmeal, salt, black pepper

Bring a pot of water to a low boil. Add cornmeal to the boiling water a handful at a time by letting it sift through your fingers, stirring with your other hand as you do this. Keep stirring and adding cornmeal until the polenta reaches a consistency heavy enough to hold a wooden spoon upright in the pot. Add salt and pepper to taste. The consistency may vary according to the dish you are serving it with or your personal taste. You may like it firmer with a tomato sauce, or, if you serve it with game, you may want it softer. If you have polenta with mushrooms or vegetables, which are more delicate, it is good almost runny.

Pasta, That's All

My brothers and I would always come home from school starving to death, but we had to wait to eat until my father came home from work. When it grew late, my mother got hungry, too. We would sit at the table with empty plates in front of us and nothing to do while my mother stood at the window looking out at the street, waiting for my father. He would leave the car at the corner and walk the rest of the way to the house. One day we asked, "Mamma, what are you doing at the window?" And she said, "I'm looking for your father's shoes so I can throw the pasta in the water." When she saw the first bit of shoe come around the corner, she would put the pasta on, and by the time he got home the pasta was cooked to perfection—al dente.

Pasta needs to be cooked in plenty of fast-boiling water. There has to be enough water in the pot so the pasta can swim around freely. Add salt once the water is boiling. And before you start to make any sauce, have a pot of water boiling slowly nearby, so you can cook the pasta when the sauce is almost ready.

To judge whether or not the pasta is cooked enough, lift out one piece and break it with your fingernail. If it feels too hard, it's not cooked enough. You can test it the same way with your teeth; that is what we call al dente. When it feels pleasurable to the touch of your teeth, the pasta is ready—not too soft, not too hard, right in between.

In Tuscan cooking, the sauces are incorporated into the pasta instead of remaining on top like a liquid garnish. To do this, we put the pasta and the sauce together in a different manner than do other Italians. Once the pasta is cooked, drain it and then add it very quickly to the pan that the sauce is in, while they are both hot. In this way, the pores of the pasta can absorb the taste of the sauce, and the flavor will spread through out. If you are adding Parmesan, do it while everything is still in the pan, and toss. It will further tie the sauce to the pasta.

When you buy Parmesan cheese, always make sure you get a piece of the crust. First, the crust has the name of the cheese printed on it, and it tells you where it comes from. You don't want an industrially produced American Parmesan cheese, which lacks the texture and taste of the genuine product from Parma. Second, the crust is excellent grated and used in cooking or combined with the center of the cheese and grated on top of pasta. Just scrape the printing off with a sharp knife. Stores usually keep the crusts for themselves and sell them as ready-made grated cheese, but it's better if you combine the crust with the

THE WISDOM OF TUSCANY

pulp and grate it yourself.

You don't have to keep Parmesan cheese in the refrigerator unless you're storing it for a long time. In my restaurant I dampen a piece of cheesecloth and wrap it around the cheese so it keeps the moisture inside. If you want to refrigerate the Parmesan, cover the damp cheesecloth with plastic wrap and it will stay indefinitely. But Parmesan cheese is not something you want to buy in large quantities. As soon as you taste it, you want to finish it.

Tagliatelle All'Ortolana
Fresh Egg Noodles With Flavors of the Kitchen Garden

Any pasta can be used here except pappardelle—it's too thick. Penne or even spaghetti are all right. (I never use linguine in any recipe. Linguine is a southern Italian pasta that we don't use in Tuscany; we use round spaghetti.) This recipe is good year-round because the vegetables can be changed according to the season.

In certain dishes, like this one, the vegetables need to be cut by hand. I always use a mezzaluna, the half-moon-shaped knife, because I like to see the imperfections of the slices. When a machine is used for cutting, chopping, or slicing, the violent power inside the machine makes the vegetables fall apart and lose their consistency when they are cooked. They taste good enough, but the presence of the whole vegetable is gone.

Pantry: Olive oil, salt, black pepper
Cold Storage: Chopped red onions, chicken or vegetable

broth, grated Parmesan cheese, butter (see note)

Market: Any combination of the following vegetables: fresh fava beans, eggplant, spinach, zucchini, asparagus, artichoke hearts, broccoli florets, carrots, Swiss chard, fresh tomatoes, fresh herbs of your choice: mint, sage, oregano, parsley, basil, tagliatelle (fresh, if available)

Heat olive oil in a pan and sauté onions over medium heat until golden. When the onions are done, add the fava beans; eggplant, peeled and cut into bite-sized pieces; spinach, roughly cut; and zucchini, cut into bite-sized pieces. Season with salt and pepper, turn the heat to low, and continue to cook and stir until vegetables are tender but still crisp. If vegetables begin to dry out, add some broth. When almost cooked, add the asparagus, par-boiled and cut into bite-sized pieces; artichoke hearts, steamed and quartered; broccoli florets, steamed; carrots, cut into ovals and steamed; or Swiss chard, shredded and sautéed. Add just enough tomatoes to give some color, then add whatever herbs you are using.

Cook the pasta until al dente in boiling water and drain. Add to vegetables, along with the Parmesan cheese and butter. Mix thoroughly over low heat and serve with additional Parmesan cheese on the side.

Note: Replace olive oil with butter throughout the preparation if you prefer a richer dish.

Penne Alla Rozza
Quill-Shaped Pasta With Rude Sauce

In this recipe, rude refers to the rough and uneven combination of the vegetables and meat. Even though the ingredients seem to be combined casually, the dish is a result of confidence in the final outcome.

Pantry: Dried porcini, olive oil, bay leaf, chopped almost to a powder, red wine, canned tomatoes, smashed in their own juice, penne, black pepper
Cold Storage: Chopped celery, thickly sliced red onion, grated Parmesan cheese, butter
Market: Prosciutto, fairly thick, in strips

Soak porcini in warm water for at least 30 minutes, then drain, squeeze dry, and chop. Set aside.

Heat olive oil in a pan and add prosciutto, celery, and onion. Cook over very low heat and when the vegetables begin to soften, add the porcini and continue to cook. When the mixture begins to smell like something very good is going on, it's time to add the bay leaf and a generous amount of wine. Then add the tomatoes. Cook over high heat for a few minutes to give the flavors a chance to combine, then lower the heat and cook slowly, partially covered, for about 30 minutes.

Meanwhile, cook the penne in boiling water until al dente, drain, and stir it into the sauce along with Parmesan and a tiny bit of butter. If you see that the sauce is too dry, add a little more butter and mix. When you serve the pasta, grind some black pepper over the top, but do not cook the pepper in the sauce because it makes the prosciutto acidic and changes the taste of the dish.

Spaghetti Alla Pirata
Spaghetti, Pirate-Style

Pantry: Olive oil, crushed red pepper, good quality white wine, canned tomatoes smashed in their own juice, spaghetti
Cold Storage: Garlic, smashed
Market: Shrimp, mussels, any available medium-sized clams, squid

Clean the shrimp, mussels, and clams and take them out of their shells. If the shrimp are large, chop them. Slice the squid into rings.

Heat olive oil in a large pan and sauté the garlic over medium heat until it is golden. Take it out and add the seafood. Cook over high heat for about 5 minutes, until the taste of the olive oil and garlic has been absorbed. Add red pepper to taste and pour in 2 glasses of wine. Let the wine reduce, then add enough tomatoes to cover the seafood. Still over high heat, bring the sauce to a boil, then turn the heat down to medium-low and reduce the sauce to half its quantity. This will take about 30 to 45 minutes. If sauce gets too dry, add a little bit of cold water.

Meanwhile, cook the pasta in boiling water until al dente, drain it, and add to the pan. Mix together and serve.

Maremma

Maremma is the most harmonious area of Tuscany. There are mountains, beaches, hills, and fields—anything you could ever want. Even though Maremma was once acquitrino, a land of marsh and quicksand, today it is a wild, earthy, fertile rich province.

People in Maremma have a hard and deep way of looking at you when they don't know you, but then they come out with a very beautiful smile that lets you know there's really a warm person behind there.

In Maremma, the hospitality is the kind that when your friends say, "Stop by and see me," they mean you have to stay for one whole meal or at least a snack. You've got to eat. Not eating something is out of the question.

Spaghetti Alla Maremmana
Spaghetti, Maremma-Style

This is a dish special to the Maremma region of Tuscany. Within this area, which is only a hundred kilometers long and forty wide, I've seen this dish made in five or six different versions because of the imaginative way the people cook. Any recipe with "Maremma" in the name has a very strong, sharp taste. This recipe is made with few ingredients, but all of them have strong flavors. I love to use spaghetti for this dish, but you can use penne as well. Pecorino cheese is better than Parmesan here because it's sharper. The dish can be made in any season. In the summertime, use really fresh, ripe tomatoes, which you just chop up and throw in, let cook, and mix.

Pantry: Olive oil, salt, black pepper, red wine, canned tomatoes smashed in their own juice (or fresh, in season)
Cold Storage: Garlic, smashed
Market: Fresh mushrooms, any variety, chunked, eggplant, peeled and chopped into chunks the same size as mushrooms, green peas, sweet Italian sausage, grated caciotta or pecorino cheese.

Heat the olive oil in a pan and sauté the garlic over medium heat until full of color. Remove garlic and add mushrooms, eggplant, and peas. Peel the casing off the sausage and break up the meat with your hand. Add it to the pan and continue to cook over medium heat until the ingredients combine and begin to color. Add salt and pepper to taste. Stir constantly so the mixture doesn't stick to the bottom of the pan. Turn the heat up to high, cover the mixture with red wine, mix some more and continue to cook. Enjoy the beautiful, strong smell of the sauce and the vegetables. When your nose tells you, "This is good; let's keep it like this," add the tomatoes and turn the heat down a little bit. Let the mixture cook for 20 minutes and if the sauce gets too dry, add more red wine—

just a small amount.

Meanwhile, cook the pasta in boiling water until it is al dente and drain it. Add it to the pan with the sauce, add the cheese, and mix thoroughly over low heat. Serve with additional grated cheese on the side.

Spaghetti Alle Vongole in Bianco
Spaghetti in White Clam Sauce

Pantry: Olive oil, crushed red pepper, spaghetti
Cold Storage: Garlic, sliced, fresh parsley, chopped
Market: Cherrystone, Littleneck, or Manilla clams in the shell

Let the clams sit in enough water to cover them for at least an hour and then wash them very well.

Pour enough olive oil in a deep pan to cover the bottom. Add garlic and red pepper and turn up the heat. When the oil is very, very hot, stand back and add the clams. Cover and let them steam until the shells are completely opened. Discard any clams that remain shut.

Meanwhile, cook the pasta in boiling, salted water and drain. At this point you have 2 choices. You can simply leave the clams in the shells, add the pasta, toss, and serve. Or, you can remove the clams from their shells, discard the shells, and return the clams to the pan with the water from the clams, olive oil, and garlic. Turn up the heat for a few minutes to reduce the liquid, add the cooked pasta, toss, and serve. If you do it the second way, the pasta absorbs the juice and clam taste right away and it is much more flavorful than if simply tossed with the clams in their shells.

Frittata Di Pasta
Italian Omelette With Pasta

In 1968, the students in my school went on strike. One morning at the opening of classes, we kicked out al the teachers and occupied the classrooms. It was a scary situation because the police had surrounded the school, and we knew they were going to break in. By early afternoon tensions were high and we were preparing for a confrontation when, all of a sudden, someone at the window yelled to me, "Pino, it's your mother." I thought, "Damn it, she's always underfoot when I don't need her." There she was, standing in a crowd of policemen, holding a big picnic basket. They wouldn't let her give it to me until they checked it for arms. Although they didn't find guns, what they did find was my lunch in the form of Frittata di Pasta, fresh bread, a bottle of wine, napkins, silverware, and salt and pepper. She must have thought we were having a picnic in there. I was very embarrassed because I was already known as the student whose mother packed his book bag with richly stuffed panini every day.

The only place she didn't follow me was to jail that night. She tried, but they wouldn't let her in.

Pantry: Olive oil, leftover pasta in its sauce, salt, black pepper
Cold Storage: Eggs, beaten

Put a little olive oil in a pan set over medium heat and add all the pasta. Then put the eggs on top and let them seep down. Add salt and pepper, and when the frittata is brown on one side, turn it over and let it get brown on the other side. It comes out very crunchy.

About Fish

Choosing Fish: You can tell a really fresh fish by its gills and eyes. The gills have to be red, and the eyes still have to look alive. You know how we say in Italian, "He has the look of a dead fish?" You don't want to eat a fish that looks like that—so dead looking that it's good for nothing. It may be dead, but it should still look lively.

Cleaning Fish: Scale and clean the fish, or have it done at the fish market, but don't have it boned. When I talk about preparing a fish, I mean the *whole* fish. Never bone a fish until after it's cooked. The skin protects the fish during cooking the same way it protected the fish when it was in the water. If the fish is filleted, it tends to get dry and tough or, if you poach it, too moist. If the fish is cooked whole, the skin acts as protection from too much heat or moisture. Of course, it is possible to do all these recipes with filleted fish, but the dish is not going to taste the same. One reason people like fillet fish is because they are scared of the bones, but don't be afraid to enjoy food. When you eat fish, your tongue and your teeth will tell you if there is something in your mouth you don't want to swallow. If there is, spit it out. Anyway, it's easier to lift the bones out of fish with a fork after the fish is cooked. But check carefully before serving.

Substitutions: Dentice, spigola, cefalo, sogliole, or any other kind of Mediterranean fish mentioned in these recipes can be replaced with common U.S. fish, such as red snapper, striped bass, pompano, groper, mullet, or scrod.

Insalata Di Mare Alla Toscana
Cold Seafood Salad, Tuscan-Style

Pantry: olive, salt, black pepper, green or black olives
Cold Storage: Sliced garlic, fresh parsley, chopped, lemon juice and wedges
Market: Cherrystone, Littleneck, or Manilla clams, baby shrimp out of the shell, squid

Soak the clams in cold water until they release sand. Steam the clams until they open and remove them from their shells, discarding any that haven't opened. Strain them and set aside the broth.

In 2 separate pots, steam the shrimp and the squid until they are white and tender. Mix the clams, shrimp, and squid in enough olive oil to moisten well and place them in a bowl with the sliced garlic, parsley, lemon juice, salt, and pepper. Add some reserved clam broth and serve cold with lemon wedges and olives.

Pesce Arrosto Con Patate
Fish Roasted With Potatoes

The day of Ferragosto—the Feast of the Assumption—is a big holiday all over Italy, and I remember both my grandmother and my mother making this dish for lunch. This is a one-dish meal, excellent made at home. I can't do it in the restaurant because people would have to wait too long while it cooked. But it's worth waiting for at home.

Pantry: Olive oil, salt, black pepper
Market: Whole baby snapper, pompano, bass, or grouper: 1 pound of fish per person, minimum 4 pounds, new potatoes, cut into small chunks, rosemary (fresh, if available)

Preheat the oven to medium-hot. Have the fish cleaned and scaled, but leave the heads on. Wet the bottom and sides of a baking dish with olive oil and place the fish in it. Put the potatoes all around the fish. Tuck sprigs of rosemary all around, then sprinkle with salt, pepper, and olive oil. Roast in the oven for about 30 minutes. Check every 10 minutes too see that the potatoes don't stick to the pan. You will know when the fish is done when you penetrate it with a fork to the spine and the fork comes out easily. The potatoes should be done, too. If you are using a smaller fish, I suggest you parboil the potatoes first, so they will be done at the same time as the fish.

A Meal By the Sea

The local people who live along the coast of Tuscany make a fish stew called Cacciucco. This dish is popular from Porto Santo Stefano in the south all the way to Livorno in the north. The beaches along this coastline are bordered by a dark and thick pine woods, unbroken except for a few areas. The locals go to these areas to fish. At one time there was a wooden bungalow near Castiglion delle Pescaia—a one-room house with a big chimney. In it lived an old fisherman, a pescatore. This fisherman had his own small business making Cacciucco. At sunset he put down the nets and in the morning took them out and prepared the fish for the Cacciucco. In the winter he worked on a fishing boat for a big Italian company, but in the summer he cooked Cacciucco from his own bungalow. He had some tables beneath the overhang of his roof so diners could sit in the shade while they ate. He served it in pottery bowls, and I always wondered where he washed them—probably in sea water, which in that area is clean and pure.

If you got there and no Cacciucco was ready, you didn't mind waiting because the beach was right there and you could just lie down on the sand with a glass of the local wine. Between the sun and the wine you usually fell asleep, but you knew when your Cacciucco was ready because the smell woke you up.

He cooked the Cacciucco in a huge iron pot over a wood fire outside his bungalow. He poured some oil in this pot, then added garlic and onions, and let them cook until they were almost burnt. He started with crabs, mussels, and clams, then

257

added big chunks of fish, eel, rockfish—whatever he had. Then the other fish were put in according to size, with the small fish and shrimp left for last. He added plum tomatoes—the kind that grow like wildfire all over Tuscany—and lots of parsley. When the tomatoes started to melt together with the fish and the seasonings, and the smell started to come on strong, he covered everything with cold water and let it cook. Twenty minutes later you were in heaven.

I was young and it was great to go there in summer and have my lunch for a couple thousand lire. Years later, I went back and looked for him, but nobody was there. You could still see traces of the fires he had built, but the poor guy had died. The sad thing is there was nobody to replace him, and his Cacciucco was so good.

Il Cacciucco
Fish and Bread Stew, Tuscan-Style

Pantry: Olive oil, salt, black pepper, Fettunta
Cold Storage: Chopped garlic, coarsely chopped red onions, chopped fresh parsley,
Market: Shellfish, including clams, mussels, and shrimp, cleaned and left in their shells, a large variety of fish, including eel and small fish, boned and cut into chunks, tomatoes (fresh or canned)
Cover the bottom of a large pot with plenty of olive oil, add the onions and garlic, and sauté them over medium heat until golden. Add clams and mussels. (Everything that is strong

tasting and juicy goes in the pot first.) Next add the chunks of eels and the rest of the fish according to size—the larger ones first, then the smaller ones. And then add the shrimp. Let everything cook briefly over high heat. Season with salt and pepper and add the tomatoes. (If you are using canned tomatoes, break them into chunks and add them with their juice. If you are using fresh tomatoes, quarter them.) Add parsley, putting a small amount aside for garnish. Let everything cook until hot, then cover the mixture with cold water to stop the cooking. Bring back to a simmer and cook over low heat, uncovered, until the fish is tender. Be careful not to overcook. Start to check the mixture after it has been simmering for 10 minutes to seek if the fish is cooked. If you can penetrate it easily with a fork, it is done.

Once the Cacciucco is cooked, (which doesn't take very long because you don't want the fish to get soft and break apart), put a piece of Fettunta in each bowl, spoon the stew over it shells and all, and sprinkle with parsley.

Gamberi Alla Pescatora
Shrimp, Fisherman's Style

Pantry: Olive oil, salt, white wine, canned tomatoes, black pepper
Cold Storage: Smashed garlic, fresh chopped parsley
Market: Shrimp, in or out of the shell

Cover the bottom of a pan with olive oil and sauté garlic over medium heat until golden. Remove garlic, add shrimp, and continue to sauté until they turn white. Pour off extra olive oil, then add a pinch of salt and enough wine to just cover. Continue to cook over medium heat and, when the wine is reduced somewhat, add tomatoes, parsley, and pepper. Partially cover and cook 4 minutes or so over medium-low heat.

A Pig For All Seasons

Every year my father would have a contadino raise and butcher a pig. A huge table would be cleared to prepare the pig, and every part would be used: the blood for blood sausage; the head, ears, and feet for soppressata (an Italian salami); the ribs for spareribs; the loin for chops; the ham for prosciutto. In one or two days the whole animal was transformed, and the pig that we had been keeping in the contadino's yard was now being kept in the cellar. We would then have prosciutto in the summer and cotechino in the fall. It was wonderful.

This is how people do these things in the country and even in the cities of Tuscany. It is impossible to imagine any city person who doesn't have a connection with a contadino who can supply eggs, mushrooms, and vegetables in season. As much as we can, we like to preserve foods when they are in season, so there will always be something out of season to enjoy all year long.

During the Middle Ages, people used to preserve meats and vegetables to use in winter and whenever there was war. They would close their doors and protect themselves from starv-

ing by living off this huge amount of stored food. They could stay behind those doors forever.

Tuscans still like to protect themselves in this way. You will never find them in their houses without food. Maybe other things will be missing, but if they have to choose between having food or something else, Tuscans will always choose food.

Rostinciana
Grilled Spareribs

Pantry: Salt, black pepper, olive oil
Market: Pork spareribs

Mix some salt, pepper, and olive oil in your hand and rub each rib with the mixture, especially around the edges where the fat is. Grill the spareribs over a hot wood fire, a barbecue, or under the broiler until crisp.

Note: You can also put the spareribs in a hot oven, in a pan with just enough olive oil to cover the bottom. They will cook almost the same way as if on the grill, but it will take longer. Start checking for tenderness with a fork after about 30 minutes. If you want them crisper, pour off the excess liquid and put the ribs back in the oven until well done.

Vegetali Alla Griglia
Grilled Vegetables

My grandmother uses nettles in the fire when grilling vegetables because this plant acts as a good filter between the vegetables and the flame. It keeps the vegetables from burning and makes them smell good. I've always thought that nettles were the nastiest plant. When I was twelve, I hid in a field with my girlfriend. My first kiss, and I finished with a face full of nettles. It almost changed my mind about romance!

Anyway, this is how we grill over a wood fire in Tuscany. Lay dry wood on the bottom of a grill. Place green wood on top of the dry wood. (The green wood doesn't burn, but it creates aromatic smoke.) Brush sprigs of fresh herbs with olive oil, lay them between layers of folded chicken wire, and put this on top of the green wood. On top of the chicken wire, place vegetables brushed with olive oil. Grill until you have something that tastes and smells good.

I've started to grill many vegetables I once thought couldn't be cooked this way and, believe me, it's an undiscovered world. If vegetables are exposed to the fire for a very short time, there is a natural reaction that makes them taste great. I've tried grilling everything, even fiddlehead ferns. They taste great, steamed first and then grilled.

Grilled vegetables can be served with prosciutto or salami and are especially good with Fettunta. A large platter of assorted grilled vegetables is an excellent appetizer. Use whatever is available, season by season.

Pantry: Salt, black pepper, olive oil
Market: Any combination of vegetables

Place vegetables on a flat pan (a pizza pan works perfectly) and season with salt, pepper, and olive oil. Place under the broiler, over a wood fire, or even in a hot oven. Turn once while they cook.

Any way you cook them, these vegetables come out perfectly—moist and tasty. Of course, they are crunchier if you put them over a wood fire or under the broiler, but if that's not possible the oven is not the worst solution. Sprinkle with lemon juice or vinegar if you like.

Panzanella

Panzanella is one more example of the many ways Tuscan cooks use bread. In this recipe, the bread captures the sharp essence of the dressing and contrasts perfectly with the fresh, crisp vegetables of the salad.

Pantry: Red wine vinegar, olive oil, salt, black pepper
Cold Storage: Vegetable broth, thinly sliced red onions
Market: Day-old bread, chunked, peeled and thinly sliced cucumber, thinly sliced scallions (white part), fresh tomatoes, chunked.

Moisten the bread with cool broth and squeeze out excess liquid. Place the bread in a bowl and sprinkle with vinegar. Mix well so the bread has a chance to absorb the flavor. Put cucumbers, scallions, onion, and tomatoes in the bowl with the bread. Add olive oil, salt, and pepper to taste, if needed. Add more vinegar and oil to taste, also if needed. Refrigerate before serving. This salad can also be kept in the refrigerator and served the next day.

NOTES

CHAPTER 3

27 "Heavy Snow Hits Much of England," *BBC,* Feb. 2, 2009

29 Happiness is contagious: "Happiness 'rubs off on others,'" *BBC,* Dec. 5, 2008

CHAPTER 5

53 David Brooks, "What Life Asks of Us," *NYT,* Jan. 30, 2009

57 Benton MacKaye, *The New Exploration: A Philosophy of Regional Planning* (Appalachian Trail Conservancy, 1991)

58 "For Nearly Half of America, Grass is Greener Somewhere Else," *Pew Research Center Publications,* Jan. 29, 2009

CHAPTER 6

59 Kenneth Johnson, "Demographic Trends in Rural and Small Town America," *Reports on Rural America* (University of New Hampshire: Carsey Institute, 2006)

61 David Grann, *The Lost City of Z: A Tale of Deadly Obsession in the Amazon* (New York: Doubleday, 2009)

68 Lewis Mumford, *The Urban Prospect* (Orlando: Harcourt, Brace & World, Inc., 1968)

CHAPTER 7

85 Jared Diamond, *Guns, Germs, and Steel: The Fates of Human Societies* (New York: W.W. Norton, 2005)

86 Penny Wilson: Sean Coughlan, "Generation of Play Deprivation." *BBC News,* Sept. 25, 2007

CHAPTER 8

88 William Shakespeare, *Troilus and Cressida* (New York: Signet Classics, 2002)

90 Ralph Waldo Emerson, "Beauty," *Nature* (New York: Penguin, 2003)

93 Joseph Conrad, "Youth," *Youth, Heart of Darkness, The End of the Tether* (New York: Penguin, 1995)

CHAPTER 9

101   Sebastian Cresswell-Turner, "An Offer You Can't Refuse," *Telegraph,* Apr. 11, 2004

102   Samuel Beckett, "All That Fall," *Collected Shorter Plays of Samuel Beckett* (New York: Grove Press, 1994)

102   New Franklin, Ohio: Michael Luo, "Months After Plant Closed, Many Still Struggling," *NYT,* Feb. 9, 2009

104   Wage drop: Marc Levinson, "Living on the Edge," *Newsweek,* Nov. 4 '91; and Peter Kilborn, "Middle Class Feels Betrayed," *NYT,* Jan. 12, 1992

104   Xerox: Doron P. Levin, "Company News." *NYT,* Dec 12, 1991

104   Sears Roebuck: "Company News," *NYT,* Jan. 8, 1992

104   I.B.M.: Lisa Foderaro, "Hudson Valley reels Under Impact of I.B.M. Cuts," *NYT,* Dec. 18, 1991

104   General Motors: Daron P. Levin, "General Motors to Cut 70,000 Jobs," *NYT,* Dec. 18, 1991

105   Louis Bromfield, *At Malabar* (Baltimore: Johns Hopkins University Press, 1998)

105   Bob Herbert, "Anxious About Tomorrow," *NYT,* Sept. 1, 2007

106   George Packer, "The Ponzi State," *The New Yorker,* Feb. 9, 2009

106   Maureen Dowd, "Wall Street's Socialist Jet-Setters," *NYT,* Jan. 27, 2009

107   Colin Turnbull, *The Mountain People* (Touchstone, 1986)

109   Kenneth Johnson, "Demographic Trends in Rural and Small Town America." *Reports on Rural America* (University of New Hampshire: Carsey Institute, 2006)

111   Claire Cain Miller, "For Craft Sales, the Recession Is a Help," *NYT,* Dec. 22, 2008

CHAPTER 10

120   Louis Bromfield, *At Malabar* (Baltimore: Johns Hopkins University Press, 1998)

121   Michel de Montaigne, *The Journal of Montaigne's Travels in Italy*

127   Louis Bromfield, *Pleasant Valley* (Wooster Book Co, 2008)

CHAPTER 11

140   Mahatma Gandhi, *The Words of Gandhi* (Newmarket Press, 2001)

145   "-cide." *Oxford English Dictionary,* 11th ed. 2008

146- Farms: John Fraser Hart, *The Land That Feeds Us* (New
147   York: W.W. Norton, 1993) and Charles A. Francis, "Alternative Agriculture," *Agricultural Systems,* Vol. 39. Issue 2. 227-229, National Research Council, 1992

147 Rachel Carson, *Silent Spring* (Boston: Houghton Mifflin Company, 1962)

148 Diet: Melissa McNamara, "Diet Industry is Big Business," *CBS News*, Dec. 1, 2006

149 Damien Cave, "In Florida, Despair and Foreclosures," *NYT*, Feb. 7, 2009

152 1,100 miles per bite: Charis Conn and Henna Silverman, *What Counts: The Complete Harper's Index* (New York: Henry Holt and Company, 1991)

152 *World Resources Institute Report, 1989*

152 Goethe: qtd. in Sigmund Freud, *Civilization and its Discontents* (New York: W.W. Norton & Company, 2005)

CHAPTER 12

165 David Streitfeld, "Where Home Prices Crashed Early, Signs of a Rebound," *NYT*, May 4, 2009

165 Margot Adler, "Behind the Ever-Expanding American Dream House," All Things Considered, *NPR*, July 4, 2006

166 John Stilgoe: "Behind the Ever-Expanding American Dream House"

169 Henry David Thoreau, *Walden* (New York: W.W. Norton & Company, 1992)

171 Bittman, Batali: Mark Bittman, "So Your Kitchen Is Tiny. So What?" *NYT*, Dec. 13, 2008

CHAPTER 15

193   Spread of happiness test: "Happiness 'rubs off on others,'" *BBC,* Dec. 5, 2008

CHAPTER 16

197   *National Women's Health Report* qtd. in "Aging: Myths vs. Facts," *NBC*

CHAPTER 17

206   Nancy Franklin, "A Place Called Hope," On Television, *The New Yorker,* Feb. 2, 2009

CHAPTER 18

213   Bob Herbert, "Magical Thinking - Stop Being Stupid," *NYT,* Dec. 26, 2008
214   Paul Krugman, "The Conscience of a Liberal," *NYT*
216   Alex Kotlowitz, "All Boarded Up," *NYT,* Mar. 8, 2009
216   "Mortgage Forgiven for 90-Year-Old Who Shot Self," *The Associated Press,* Oct. 5, 2008
217   Hervey Cleckley/ Robert Hare: John Seabrook, "Suffering Souls: The Search for the Roots of Psychopathy," *The New Yorker,* Nov. 10, 2008
217   Nick Paumgarten, "The Pits," Department of Visualization, *The New Yorker,* Dec. 8, 2008

218 GM Chairman: Dana Mattioli, "GM CEO Wagoner Regrets Lutz' Global Warming Comments," *Wall Street Journal,* Mar. 11, 2008

CHAPTER 18

221 John Berger, *Pig Earth* (New York: Vintage, 1992)

222 Beverly Smith, "More a Way of Life," *The Globe and Mail,* Dec. 28, 1991

224 Carl Jung, *Symbols of Transformation* (Princeton: Princeton University Press, 1977)

225 Stucco ghettos: George Packer, "The Ponzi State," A Reporter at Large, *The New Yorker,* Feb. 9, 2009

225 Alexis de Tocqueville, *Democracy in America* (New York: Penguin, 2003)

227 Burkhard Bilger, "The Long Dig," A Reporter at Large, *The New Yorker,* Sept. 15, 2008